WOODY BAY

Woody Bay, lime kiln and cottage by Ian Hudson, 1990.

WOODY BAY

Harriet Bridle

MERLIN BOOKS LTD.
Braunton Devon

First published in Great Britain 1991

British Library Cataloguing in Publication Data
Bridle, Harriet
Woody Bay.
1. (District) Devon. North Devon. Woody Bay. Description & travel
I. Title
914.2352

ISBN 0 86303 510-8

ISBN 0 86303 510-8
Printed in England by Antony Rowe Ltd., Chippenham, Wilts.

This book is for all who love wild, grand and lonely places for they are sure to appreciate beautiful Woody Bay. The author aims to give the 'feel' of this remote North Devon inlet together with its historical background. The book offers literary and artistic views of the bay and the local area seen through the eyes of other writers and artists in the past and present. *Woody Bay* also presents miniature portraits and reminiscences of local people. It describes the renowned Lynton & Barnstaple Railway and touches on folklore and other similar unusual subjects. There is a good selection of photographs relating to all these aspects. Each chapter is designed to be complete in itself. It is the first book to be written about haunting Woody Bay which is a hamlet in Martinhoe. The author hopes it will have both a serious and a more popular appeal.

Harriet Bridle was born in Malta and is a naval Captain's daughter. She was educated at a variety of schools, principally at St Swithun's School, Winchester. Later in life she gained an Open University BA degree in History and English.

On leaving school, the author was employed for a short time as a publisher's secretary in London. Then she worked in a boys' club in Bermondsey before undertaking a course in Social Science at Southampton University. At Southampton she played lacrosse for the Combined Universities and for the South-West of England.

She was married in 1962 and had four children. She worked in boarding-schools for a number of years.

For twenty years her home has been in Woody Bay where she has taken a keen interest in local history. She belongs to a number of local associations and a local church and enjoys many different outdoor pursuits, especially walking and exploring the Devon and Exmoor countryside.

For
MARK, RACHEL, *and* DEBORAH
and in memory of
JONATHAN

CONTENTS

ACKNOWLEDGEMENTS

I would like to thank all those who helped and encouraged me with the writing and production of *Woody Bay*. Particularly, I would like to thank Lawrie Scott and Colin and O-lan Style, the latter for their interesting research into the history of the Woody Bay Hotel which led me on many a fascinating trail; Don Bennett, John Travis, George Owen, David Kester Webb and Steve Mulberry, the National Trust Warden for Woody Bay, for their information and advice; Noel Allen of Alcombe Books, Minehead, Peter Hames and Tarka Books, Barnstaple, Arthur Berry of Lynton, Porcupines, the Heaths of Torridge Books, Langtree and Rothwell and Dunworth; the Shaplands and Derek Crush of Barnstaple for their help in obtaining old postcards; the Devon Record Office, Exeter and the North Devon Library, Record Office and Athenaeum, Barnstaple and all those I talked to connected with Woody Bay, some of whom are mentioned in the text, and who generously passed on facts, fiction and ideas. My thanks are also due to the patience and understanding of Mr and Mrs Derek Stockwell of Merlin Books. I owe special appreciation to Brian Pearce of the Exmoor National Park who meticulously photographed a substantial number of the illustrations in the book and who advised me on the finer points of natural history; and to John Oldham for lending me the unpublished history of Martinhoe and photograph album compiled by his grandfather, the Reverend Reginald Walter Oldham, Rector of Martinhoe from 1886-1927 and for magnanimously allowing me to use these freely; and also to Dr Ernest Mold of Lynton for kindly letting me borrow and use as a source his as yet unpublished history of Lynton and for lending me some very interesting climbing papers. I am extremely grateful to friends who read my text and made many helpful comments and suggestions, especially Anne Born, my tutor at the Arvon Centre at Totleigh Barton, and Margaret A. Reed and not least Jenny Davis and others of the Eden Centre, Lynton. Any mistakes and omissions are my own and I would be glad to hear from any reader who cares to suggest corrections or additions to my material. Finally, I must thank my long-suffering family, especially Ron, who initiated me into the mysteries of the Amstrad.

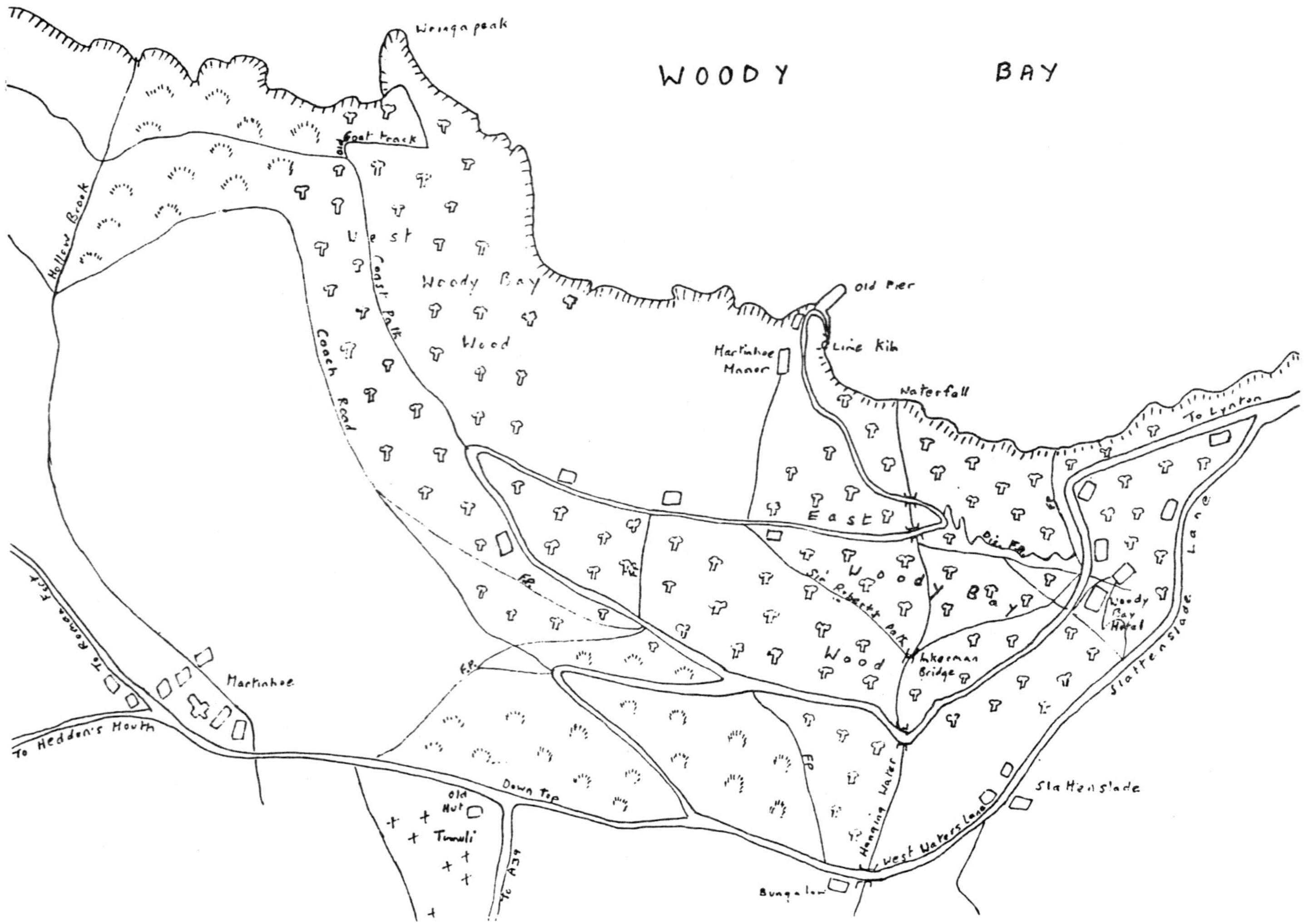
WOODY BAY
Wringapeak
Goat track
Hollow Brook
West Woody Bay Wood
Coast Path
Coach Road
Old Pier
Lime Kiln
Martinhoe Manor
Waterfall
To Lynton
East Woody Bay Wood
Sir Robert's Path
Woody Bay Hotel
Lane
Slattenslade
Bridge
Hanging Water
West Waters Lane
Bungalow
Martinhoe
To Heddon's Mouth
Down Top
Old Hut
Tumuli
to A39
F.P.

CHAPTER ONE

FIRST IMPRESSIONS

Woody Bay sweeps in a magnificent curve, its grandeur strikes and haunts the eye and heart and mind. The eye traverses rocks and boulders and the flat-topped cliff of Crock Point, swings round and climbs to the pinnacle of the sheer, and sometimes vertical, hog's-backed heights of 800 feet or more. Beyond Crock Point is Duty Point and its tower, Lee Abbey, and behind them, the Valley of Rocks. Out at sea, the often turbulent Lynmouth race can be seen.

Exmoor is a high plateau and her cliffs are among the highest in England. The cliffs at Woody Bay consist of Lynton Slates (the oldest exposed rocks in North Devon) overlain by Hangman Grits. From about 395 million years ago, sedimentation of rocks was occurring partly under the sea during the Lower and Middle Devonian period eventually producing the fantastic North Devon cliffs of Exmoor. The structure of these cliffs can be amply studied from the foreshore of Woody Bay. There are a small number of fossil species in the Lynton Beds which, because the rocks are so friable, are difficult to extract whole. Amongst other minerals found at Woody Bay are the common calcite and quartz, gleaming silver-white.[1-6]

There are caves, there are climbs, amidst breath-taking colours of buff, white, grey, ochre, rust-brown, burnt-black, rose-red, maroon, purple and greens of every hue. Climbing up to the tip of the outcrop of Crock Point is quite a daring feat, as half-way up there is a huge 'step' to be mounted. Nearer the beach there is an old worn-away track running up to the private green field above Crock Point. It was the old fishermen's path from Lee Bay: it was the farmer's way down to the beach from his homestead, part of which fell over the cliff in the last century, and the path which coastguards and firemen used to rescue visitors cut off by the tide. The track leads on to what, I fancy, is the old remaining patch of the farmer's garden and his gateway. Interesting rock pools are revealed at low tide near Crock Point and here, too, lies the lovely, almost deserted far beach with its restful sandscape. (It is a good half-hour's tough clamber over the boulders to reach from the main beach.)

The most interesting cave is not far from here towards the inhabited part of Woody Bay. The cave has a largish hollow opening from which there is a blissful view of the east end of the Bay. On past copper-coloured landslides, bringing in their wake whitened trees, some cracks may be spotted running right up the umber cliffs. There are thin waterfalls dribbling down vertical gullies and several can be heard but not seen. Seagulls wheel angrily as strollers go by. They nest on huge boulders fallen long ago from the towering cliffs.

Wild Woody Bay is for the connoisseur of nature, of the elements, of shadowy fragmented history, of contemplation and of solitude.

Perhaps the feature which is the crowning glory of Woody Bay is the Hanging Water Fall. Such falls, which help to make the North Devon coast so special, are a feature rarely to be seen in Great Britain.[3] The Hanging Water dashes downward making tier upon tier of cascading waterfalls of clear fresh water, falling precipitously on to the main beach where it rushes to join the salty sea. It can vary, however, from a torrent to a trickle depending on the rainfall, and though never warm, in the coldest weather it can become almost ice-bound, encrusted with huge icicles on either side. Children (and adults) play in it, teenagers cool off under it, babies are washed in it and hippies have been seen to shampoo their tangled locks beneath its spray. In the winter storms of 1990 a landslip occurred on the east side of the Hanging Water Fall taking away the face of the cliff there and exposing a sheet of bare pink rock.

The other great feature of the Bay, apart from the mighty cliffs and long natural waterfall, must be the oaks which cling tenaciously to massive heights and continue down to the sea in great profusion. It seems that Devon excels in the exuberance of trees reaching beach-level.[7] In 1981 my neighbour at Hawks Hill Cottage observed a whirlwind felling acres of trees in a single stroke.

The colours of Woody Bay are forever changing according to the time of day and the mood of the weather. The rose-pink of the dawn sky switches to the ethereal white light of the evening. The sea varies from a soft, quiet millpond to an angry, stormy monster. Pale blue becomes turquoise and duck egg, then perhaps a rich deep blue and oft-times the colour of the sea is a facsimile of the green of the enfolding oaks above. Sometimes it is the hue of cloudy slate grey which may turn to the rose and silver of a sunny evening.

The sea in the Bay needs to be respected: the tides rise up to 11½ metres so the whole beach is cleaned twice daily. The sea comes in rapidly, which means that walkers can be cut off easily by the tide if they are not watchful and it is difficult, especially in rough weather, to launch and beach boats. There are jagged, barnacle-clad rocks for the unsuspecting swimmer or boatman to scrape against at high tide. There is a relentless diagonal current crashing the waves on to the beach with particular, irregular vehemence when the wind is fierce and there is a strong undertow westwards when the tide is going out. I had great difficulty on one such occasion swimming back from Woody Bay private beach and had a hard task struggling round the pier base to the main beach. I was revived with a glass of wine proffered to me by a bookseller acquaintance, who had watched my efforts from above at Woody Bay Cottage where he was staying.

Most of the boats which come into Woody Bay are the local fishing boats from Lynmouth, seeking mainly mackerel. Yachts, often with white sails and colourful spinnakers, sometimes anchor in the Bay when the sea is calm. There are also holiday-makers' rubber dinghies and one or two vessels belonging to residents. Further out in the channel merchant and naval shipping both anchor and pass by. Pleasure steamers chug past the Bay and smaller boats for trippers give their passengers a taste of the rocky, cave-ridden Exmoor coast.

The 'private' beach is much smaller than the main beach. The only pedestrian access to it is via manor land, or by way of a scramble from the old pier when the tide is going out. But it, too, has jutting cliffs and rocks backing it and huge boulders strewn around at random. Gulls nest on the former. There used to be a precipitous path down to the private shore beneath West Woody Bay Wood, but now it has been largely obliterated by storm damage. From the pier head the next point westwards is Wringapeak which is very sheer. Round the corner is its dramatic hollow tip, on the top of which on a grassy patch lies a squat stone circle, thought to be of modern origin. A hair-raising track clings round the edge of West Wringapeak cliffs, separated from a vertical drop only by a frail scrub hedge down to slippery grass and slanting boulders. This leads either up to the wind-blown top of Wringapeak, via a narrow escarpment, or downwards over and under massive boulders (which makes for a tight squeeze) to Wringapeak beach. It is possible for experienced and wary rock scramblers and climbers at low spring tides to clamber to Hollowbrook from Woody Bay via Wringapeak. But the Woody Bay cliffs are dangerous to scale. Wringapeak is a marvellously deserted and secret spot.

There are many species of trees, shrubs, and creepers and there is a good variety of herbs and mosses in lovely Woody Bay. Besides the oaks with their young leaves in delicate shades of pink and gold at the height of summer, there are striking mountain ash trees with their brilliant red berries and in early summer the Wood can be ablaze with wild rhododendrons. Snowberry, blackberry, wild raspberry and strawberry, nightshade, bindweed, buddleia, ivy, bryony and dogrose flourish. Lichens can be found on the trees. *Usnea articulata* which only grows in areas with pure air has been seen in three places on Exmoor, according to Noel Allen, the Exmoor naturalist.

Here, too, is the infamous Himalayan knotweed. A local clergyman (possibly the Revd J. F. Chanter of Parracombe)[8] is said to have sprinkled seeds of *polygonum polystachyum* on the banks of the old Lynton & Barnstaple railway line, thinking they were somewhat bare. Residents have spent time and money since the seeds sprouted trying to rid the Bay of this unwelcome, tenacious weed; apparently it has roots as thick as a man's arm going down as deep as the soil up to 40 feet. Strong weed-killer is expensive and damaging to local water sources if used near the latter, and cutting and recutting is a time-consuming process. But it is heart-breaking to see this Himalayan jungle weed growing down the hillsides, overwhelming the native plants. I remember the field beneath my cottage when it was filled with willowherb, red campion, foxglove, ragwort and other wild flowers. Now few flowering plants remain besides the pernicious knotweed.

On Woody Bay beach there are seaweeds of many varieties and on the rocks a vivid yellow ochre lichen grows extensively.

As well as those already mentioned, the flowers include bugle, nettle, sea-pink, honeysuckle, montbretia, cow- and greater bur-parsley, alexanders, toadflax, yellow oxalis, dragon's teeth, thistle, orchid, sorrel, wood anemone, clover, sheep's-bit, scarlet pimpernel, woodruff, ox-eye daisy, thrift, herb Robert, speedwell, cowslip, forget-me-not, violet and primrose. In spring there are tiny snowdrop and daffodil valleys near the Hanging Water. At the top of Woody Bay brilliant yellow gorse grows in abundance and purple heather and thick clusters of whortleberries.

Some unusual butterflies, including some of the blues, flutter around the Bay and especially into gardens. Besides the usual admirals and peacocks, there are other striking brown butterflies with orange, yellow, white and blue markings such as the fritillaries, hairstreaks and tortoiseshells. Less common sea birds to be spotted are the guillemot, razorbill, fulmar, oyster-catcher, rock pipit and gannet. In the woods the green woodpecker makes itself heard and the peregrine[9] can be seen. I believe there may be more birds nesting on the eastern cliffs of Woody Bay than there were twenty years ago — a sign of less human disturbance, perhaps.

Another object which flies across the Bay with some regularity is large and yellow — the welcome rescue helicopter from RAF Chivenor at Braunton. It comes, single-minded, on its mission to rescue those in North Devon and elsewhere, on the cliffs or in the sea, for whom help has been called. Many grateful folk have been winched from turbulent waters and others, more dangerously, from the cliff ledges to which they have fallen. Great is the consternation when locals are told periodically that this amenity is to be abandoned by the government. Their continual outcries have been effective so far for this proposed economic cut has been shelved since 1989 and, for the foreseeable future at least, the continuing presence of No.22 Squadron seems secure.

An idea of the importance of the RAF Rescue Helicopter Service can be gauged from the following example. A friend of mine from the Lee Abbey Community was scrambling one day along the Wringapeak ledge with a companion. To Rosemary's horror, her friend slipped and fell 300 feet down a narrow gully. The wind was strong on the cliff face and the rough seas would have prevented a sea rescue. The Chivenor crew on arrival assessed the situation. The helicopter entered the bowl from the seaward side and let out the winchman with a stretcher. He had to climb down the last section of dangerous and precipitous rock face (30 feet) to the hurt girl. She was found to have a broken thigh and probably a fractured skull. The winchman attended to her cuts and abrasions which bled profusely. He then transferred her to a stretcher with much difficulty.

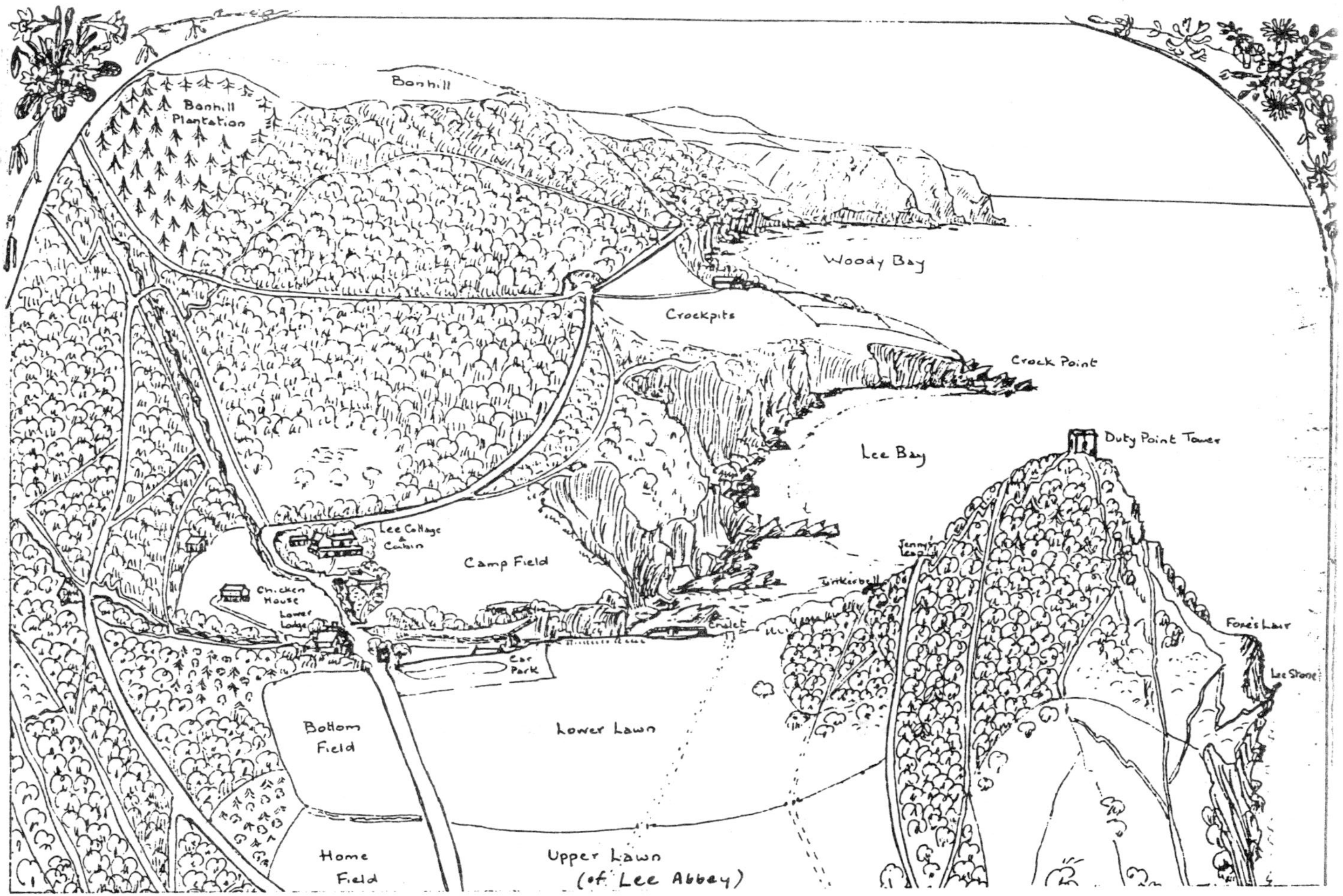

Lee Bay and Woody Bay by Ursula Kay

Because of the turbulence the pilot and navigator decided to use 120 feet of extension rope which they let down to the winchman on the ground. He had to keep his feet in contact with the rock face and consequently had the full weight of the stretcher on his arms and legs. The helicopter was only 5 feet away from the cliff face.

Once aboard, the crew flew the injured girl to the local hospital's landing-site and from there she was transferred to an ambulance.[10]

Dr Mold of Lynton was once involved in a dangerous climb locally, using rope and pitons on wet and slimy surfaces to help rescue an experienced climber. C. H. Archer had broken his thigh while climbing with Cyril Manning at West Lymcove Point in between Ramsey Beach and Bosley Gut below Trentishoe Church. The helicopter was unable to come in close enough to the cliff (a common occurrence on this coastline) so police and firemen had to haul Archer 1,100 feet up the cliff, tightly strapped to a stretcher. This should stand as a warning to climbers, particularly the inexperienced, attempting to climb the local cliffs. Dr Mold, who was in attendance on the injured man, administered analgesic injections to 68-year-old Archer at judged intervals.[9]

Fauna which has been spotted in the Bay includes shoals of jellyfish — for example, the compass, a large glassy-fawn type topped like a mushroom or umbrella with brown steaks down its dome. It has brown spots at the bottom of its rim and brown and filmy tentacles which sway silently in the sea beneath its hood. Twice I have seen otters in a small cove near the Hanging Water, once a mother playing with her babies. I saw my first adder on a warm sunny day during the drought of 1989 in the woods above Wringapeak. A streak of dull colours and cunning, it slithered away into thick undergrowth when I disturbed it from its coil of contentment near the head of our watercourse.

I also saw, to my great surprise, a lone seal pop its head out of the water whilst swimming in the Bay. John, the marvellous Woody Bay Hotel chef, sighted a seal right up on the beach by the swimming-pool at the end of October 1989. The seal and his dog barked at each other which brought the creature to John's notice. Another friend of mine observed porpoises in the Bristol Channel off Woody Bay as recently as two summers ago. Harmless whales and small sharks have been seen out in the channel, especially by Lynmouth boatmen.

Only on Exmoor have there always been red deer in their wild state in England, and from Exmoor they spread to the Quantocks. I have the mounted head of a deer which was shot in the Bay in 1942. Deer still haunt Woody Bay today and are to be seen frequently in the region of Wringapeak and throughout the Woody Bay woods. In 1985 Trevor Jordan began to build up a stock of animals when he bought the Manor intending to have a wildlife park there. A visitor to Woody Bay Cottage was quite astonished when, while turning a corner on an early morning walk, he was confronted by two wallabies. He thought that his eyes must be playing tricks or that he had drunk one too many the night before, despite next seeing the rather more assuring, though still unusual, sight of two deer walking on the beach road. In 1989 there was a large stag standing boldly in the middle of my next-door neighbour's vegetable patch as I was setting off one evening for a stroll. There has also been strong evidence of these richly chestnut-coloured creatures in my own garden. They favour early morning and twilight for their forages. Deer often sport themselves on manor land, sometimes in bright sunlight at midday, as bold as brass, and they racket through the trees there. In the late spring of 1990 I found my first (four atop) antler in the woods.

We entertained a tame pole cat ferret and a squirrel on separate occasions at the cottage last year. The former ran eagerly into the house while the latter forwardly jumped on to our little flat lawn frolicking about as we breakfasted there. They were missed when they left. The Exmoor beast has been sighted in the Bay, too.

Woody Bay, once Wooda Bay, is a hamlet of fifteen houses, only one of which is occupied by a family who have lived in the Bay for several generations — the farming Crangs of medieval Slattenslade. Eight of the houses in Woody Bay proper are late Victorian, two have partly Victorian structures and have been rebuilt, and one is of the twentieth century.

Woody Bay Cottage is probably the most attractive building and one of the oldest, dating from the eighteenth century. It comprises two white-washed workmen's cottages (with a Victorian wing) on a steep wall just above the beach. They were once called the Beach Cottages. Near by, the house aptly named Trees was the old post office and took in guests.[11] Less than half the households now gain their income from the holiday trade.

Most of the man-made structures on the beach and surrounds are Victorian, although the pretty limekiln was built in 1753. This was quite an early initiative to help cope with the local agrarian revolution of the eighteenth century. The kiln was used to calcine Welsh limestone for Devon's acid farmlands near by. The limekiln had a slipway down to the sea for bringing up the goods brought by boat to the land, notably limestone and coal. Pairs of low rusty spikes, or their bases, can still be discovered today at low water leading across the beach from the direction of the kiln to the sea.

In 1885 Colonel Benjamin Greene Lake (1839-1909), a London solicitor, bought the manor at Martinhoe and attempted to develop Woody Bay to make it into a second Lynmouth. He converted the principal house, known as Wooda Bay, into the Wooda Bay Hotel (which Stanley Holman rechristened the Manor House Hotel and which now is Martinhoe Manor) and included in it the Old Harbour Inn. From 1888 onwards Colonel Lake planned and built the Glen Hotel and stables (Woody Bay Hotel and Coach House), The Lodge (later The Pines and Crockpitts), Oak House (afterwards Oakhurst and The Freak and at present the White House), and Glen Villa (later Glen View and now the Red House).[12] Lake constructed 'a very fine 16-foot road from Hunter's Inn to Wooda Bay' during 1893-95 which ran over the common to Martinhoe Cross.[13] In 1896 he cut a new road to run past Glen Hotel to join the cliff road on the right-angled bend below Glen View, and he forged the coach road to Hunter's Inn.

In 1895 Benjamin Lake began to erect a pier for steamers, the first one arriving in 1897. The pier was planned to be about 100 yards long but, because of the financial difficulties, Lake had to reduce this to 80 yards. It was to have had a dog-leg extension and further outer landing-stage, starting from the north-west end of the then existing pier, which would have doubled it and facilitated the arrival of steamers in less favourable conditions. Colonel Lake also intended to build a lift like the Cliff Railway at Lynmouth, which would connect with his branch line to the Lynton & Barnstaple railway at Martinhoe Cross. What dreams! (Fervently echoed by my son, Mark, seventy years later.)

But the pier could not survive the storms of 1899 and 1900 which caused it to break up. It is rumoured in the vicinity that it was through the machinations of the locals, unable to abide Lake and his schemes, that this facility was mortally damaged with axes and finally pulled down in 1902.[14-17]

Now all that remains is a pleasing pier head, where there was once a Victorian tea-shop, and the pier foundations with the broken bases of the rusting iron girders still visible. Fishermen practise their sport on the pier head at low tide. The remaining supporting wall is sheer and massive.

Lake also built a swimming-pool amongst big rocks to the east of the Hanging Water and a ladies' changing hut. Not much remains of the latter now, but swimmers can still use the pool, which would be even better if thoughtless fun-seekers forbore to throw boulders into it. There are still faint traces of the old postman's hut and his cast-iron stove on the right-hand side of the last hairpin bend before Woody Bay Cottage.

Like most of the houses in the Bay, Trees, once the post office and situated near the postman's hut, has had a number of owners in the twentieth century. Today it boasts a pop star, Elkie Brooks, who lives there with her husband and two little boys. Wringapeak, until recently, was owned by David Tench of legal, media and Consumer Association fame.

Another celebrated person who lived at Martinhoe (in the parish of which lies Woody Bay) in the nineteenth century was (Bishop) James Hannington. He was a curate at the church and was renowned for his pastoral care, the cutting of dangerous cliff paths and for wearing yellow breeches and gaiters. His bishop told him, "You've got fine legs I see; mind you run about your parish."[18]

The National Trust bought 120 acres of the Woody Bay Manor estate in 1965, thus preserving the scenery and character of the Bay in perpetuity. It was one of the first properties acquired under the Enterprise Neptune scheme. The Devon County Council and the Exmoor Society also gave financial help.

Woody Bay is important biologically not only because of its coastal hanging oak woods, with its sessile oaks therein and other interesting and rare tree species such as yew and whitebeam respectively, but also because of its important sea bird nesting colonies. The coastal views are, all agree, spectacular and the property is backed by moorland.

The National Trust, with not unlimited resources, has made a good job of stewarding Woody Bay since 1965. It cares for the woods and wildlife and faces a continuous battle with the twin invasive weeds, rhododendron and Himalayan knotweed. In 1988 the Trust restored the cobbled slipway to the beach, the limekiln and the old sea-wall. And in 1989 the acquisition of the Highveer cliffs to the west of Woody Bay joins the Bay to the rest of the Trust's west Exmoor Estate, now totalling 2,000 acres of England's most dramatic coast. The beach road needs to be kept nicely for those who use it, for what lies on either side by way of woodlands and rough fields sloping down to the cliffs, beach and sea is Woody Bay wonderland.[19]

References to Chapter One

1. *The North Devon Hand-Book* The Revd George Tugwell (1877) Simpkin, Marshall & Co.
2. *The Coast Scenery of North Devon* E. A. Newell Arber (1911) reprinted 1969 Kingsmead Reprints.
3. *The North Devon Coast* S. H. Burton (1953) Werner Laurie.
4. *Devon* W. G. Hoskins (1954) Collins.
5. *Exmoor National Park* ed. John Coleman-Cooke (1974) HMSO.
6. 'Geology of the country around Ilfracombe and Barnstaple' *British Geological Survey* E. A. Edmonds, A. Whittaker and B. J. Williams (1985) HMSO.
7. *Unknown Devon* L. du Garde Peach (1927) Bodley Head.
8. *The Lynton and Barnstaple Railway* G. A. Brown, J.D.C. Prideaux and H. G. Radcliffe (1964) David & Charles.
9. *Coastal Climbs in North Devon* C. H. Archer Supplement for 1963/1965 — private paper.
10. *RAF News* Squadron Leader John Weaver (late 1960s).
11. *The Homeland Handbooks Lynton and Lynmouth* vol.37 (*c.*1920).
12. The Valuation Lists 1888-1911 and Rate Books 1893-1911 of Martinhoe in the possession of the Chairman of the Parish Meeting, Mr Reg Dallyn.
13. *Ilfracombe Gazette and Observer* (15.10.1895).
14. *Ships and Harbours of Exmoor* Graham Farr (1970) E.P.
15. Papers and photos of R. W. and M. S. Oldham late 19th & 20th centuries.
16. Plan and Section Wooda Bay pier 24.11.1888.
17. *Exmoor in the Old Days* Rosemary Ann Lauder (1984) Bossiney Books.
18. *James Hannington — A History Of His Life and Work* E. C. Dawson (1887) Seeley & Co.
19. National Trust guides to Woody Bay and the Heddon Valley and the *N. T. Biological Survey* September 1979.

CHAPTER TWO

SOCIAL HISTORY

The parish registers of Martinhoe date from 1632, although no one is recorded therein living at Whiddiby, Weddebay, Withy Bay or Wooda Bay before 1814. This may be due to the fact that the forms for the registers were first printed requiring specific details in 1813. The Courtney estate books from 1662 are still in existence with details of leases of land including those in Mattinhow. Martinhoe was owned by the Courtneys and their descendants for most of the eighteenth and nineteenth centuries. By 1733 Mary Paston and Elizabeth Chichester were co-heiresses of the Courtney estates on the decease of John Courtney Esq. Mary, the daughter of John Courtney, had married William Paston. Around 1750 their daughter, Anna Maria Paston, married George Throckmorton, the son of Sir Robert Throckmorton. At this time there were Lords and Blackmores at Slattenslade and Sloleys at Martinhoe.

In 1753 a lease agreement was made between 'John Chichester of Arlington Esq. and Elizabeth his wife and William Dewey of Arlington, gent.', in consideration of a 'limekiln and buildings in erecting at or near the lower part of Whiddiby with twelve acres of the common or waste ground adjoining the said kiln, to be enclosed from the other part of the said common'. The lease was for seventy years and the payment involved was a Portuguese coin called a doublejohn and £26.8s., and the rent was 2s.6d.

The buildings in question may have been a dwelling house where Martinhoe Manor now is, or the Wooda Bay cottages together with huts needed in connection with the limekiln, or a combination of all three.

Land and property was owned, at least as leasehold, and occupied by a succession of the same close-knit local families in Martinhoe during the late eighteenth and early nineteenth centuries except, it appears, for one year, according to the Land Tax Records. In 1784 Mrs Anna Maria Throckmorton, the widow of George Throckmorton Esq., entered the lists as the owner of most of Martinhoe. (In 1775 an account of books and papers belonging to several manors of Mrs A. M. Throckmorton was made, including references to her estate at Martinhoe.) After 1784 the names of the leaseholders only were ascribed to the apportionments.

The revised *Risdon* in 1811 recorded that George Courtney of Molland owned Martinhoe manor and the *Magna Britannia* of 1822 confirmed that he was still the owner.

In 1823 an assignment was undertaken between William Dovell, probably the brother of the rector, Joseph Dovell, and Messrs Dovell, Blackmore and Roberts concerning, amongst other 'leaseholds, messuages and tenements in Martinhoe, Devon', a dwelling house and about eight acres of common at Weddebay and one limekiln. The Weddebay entitlements had belonged to George Lovering and, in 1823, were in the possession of William Dovell and tenants. The schedule of the tithe apportionments of 1840 termed William Dovell the occupier of 'Weddebays and Lime Kiln'.

There is scant record of people, property or cultivated land in Woody Bay before 1800. James Squire was the first person ascribed to 'Withy Bay' in the parish registers. He married Ann Lord in 1812 and his daughter Mary was baptized at Martinhoe church in 1814. In successive baptismal entries James was called a labourer and then a farmer who resided at 'Withy Bay'. This was a fairly standard occupational synonym at the time. Poor Mary later had an illegitimate daughter who was baptized Temperance in 1837.

The other two families mentioned in the parish registers in the early part of the nineteenth century were the Jones and the Streets. Richard and Mary Jones lived at 'Withy Bay' when their son, Daniel, was baptized in 1838. The other couple were William and Elizabeth Street who were there in 1842.

These three couples must have lived in the old building standing on the site of Martinhoe Manor, the present manor house, and at the cottages by the sea.

Ann Lord and Richard Jones were likely to have been relatives of the families who farmed Slattenslade in the eighteenth and early nineteenth centuries.

A certain Philip Squire was mentioned in the Land Tax Records of 1780-1832. He resided at Bonhill from 1814-16 and may well have been a relative of James. Both Squires would have seen the results of the 1814 Crock Pits landslip when, according to a record in a scrap-book in the Martinhoe parish file at the North Devon Athenaeum, Barnstaple, a large crack of eighty yards long and six feet wide appeared when nine acres were displaced. Farmer Bromham was the tenant of the land which belonged to Arundel Yeo.

When the Great Tithe Survey was undertaken in the 1840s, Sir Robert George Throckmorton, baronet, from Warwickshire, presumably the son of Mrs George Throckmorton, owned Martinhoe manor and most of Martinhoe. The tithe map shows a house where Martinhoe Manor now stands. In the schedule Sir Robert was termed the occupier 'Himself' of the 'Woods'.

In 1859 a most interesting 'lease to a piece or parcel of land at Wooda Bay in Martinhoe, Devon for building purposes' was agreed. This lease was from Sir Robert George Throckmorton to Thomas Geen of Lynmouth, builder. The particulars of the lease referred to an 'old cottage' on the land in question. The new house to be built was to be Wooda Bay house, and an accompanying map or plan showed both the house and cottage. Martinhoe Manor has a Victorian exterior but inside there is evidence of an earlier house. There are thick walls, an old cupboard, chimney and fireplace, and old windows in one of the bedrooms. An earlier entrance, which is now the doorway to the bar, was at one time the front door.

If there was a manor house in Woody Bay before Sir Robert George Throckmorton owned the estate, it does not appear to be marked on the OS map of 1809 and there was no mention of it in Risdon's *Survey* of 1811. Nor was it substantial enough to be included in White's *History of Devonshire* (1850) nor to be recorded in Billing's *Directory of Devon* of 1857. A house on the site of the present Martinhoe Manor is first seen on the tithe map of 1840 and in an engraving by G. Rowe of Cheltenham produced about the same time, where it appears as a much smaller building. It is shown on the map which was part of the sale indenture of 1859. However, as Sir Robert apparently rebuilt the house in 1859, the original building was probably an old farmhouse (such as Hugh Wichehalse found at Ley Bay when fleeing from the plague in Barnstaple two centuries earlier).

In 1862 Nicholas William Throckmorton, Sir Robert's eldest surviving son, became lord of the manor. His son, William Throckmorton, owner of the Molland estate, succeeded to the title in 1870.[1]

In 1872 William Ayshford Sanford JP (1818-1902) of Nynehead Court, nr. Wellington, Somerset took the lease of 'the lands to Wooda Bay with residence and shootings over the *whole* of the property . . . for 20 years at £100 per annum'. Mr Sanford was charged a low rent because he was to make additions and, indeed, in 1873 he enlarged the house.[2] This was the summer home of William Sanford's family. His father, Edward A. Sanford, was the second generation owner of Lynton Cottage, Lynton. The family evidently had the knack of finding the most beautiful coastline views when choosing their homes.

Both William and his brother, Henry, worked for some years in Australia in the mid-nineteenth century. Their sister, Henrietta Mary, married Edward Lewis Knight, brother of Frederic Knight of Simonsbath, and their children became heirs of the latter.

William Sanford was married twice, first in 1857 to Sarah Ellen Seymour who died in 1867, and then in 1874 to Sarah Elizabeth Harriett Hervey and she died in 1877.

The principal house at Wooda Bay was sometimes let by the Sanfords, probably especially after William Sanford's second wife died. A bailiff was permanently in residence. There was a yacht there, horses and poultry and a walled garden with good vegetables. Around 1880 'the four-in-hand went from Nynehead to Woody Bay'.[3]

The census of 1841 recorded that Bartholomew Delbridge aged 60 was an agricultural labourer at Wooda Bay, living there with his wife Elizabeth (55), and their son John (18), and daughter Joanna (11). The census also confirmed that James Squire was working then as an agricultural worker at Wooda Bay and lived in the bay with his wife and three daughters.

In 1851 the Delbridge family was still there and son John was an agricultural labourer like his father, but Joanna was absent from this census. James Squire was still working, though listed as a widower, and two daughters remained with him. Ten years later Walter Tebbitt was in residence with his wife, two sons and two servants. Mr Tebbitt's occupation was that of fund holder which probably meant he had a pension or some other private means. It is just possible that he may have been in charge of Sir Robert Throckmorton's local estate finances. Thomas Morris was the agricultural labourer with his wife, daughter Dorcas, who was a house servant, and son John, a carter.

John Delbridge (whose relations lived at Leymouth) returned in the 1871 census. Joanna Delbridge also reappeared as John's wife. John was 51 and Joanna 41, according to the census. Could she have been his (adopted) sister of the 1841 census or was she another Joanna altogether? John was a lime-burner in 1871 and he and Joanna had six sons. William (19) was a farm servant. In 1881 John Delbridge was still a lime-burner, his son Richard (23) was a seaman and another son Thomas (18) was a shoemaker. John's son, John junior, was ten in 1871. He was absent from the fifth census so presumably was working away from Woody Bay. From 1892-1902, according to the Martinhoe rates books, John Delbridge lived at Myrtle Cottage, either as tenant or caretaker to the owner, William Keeling, who was living at Bull Inn Chambers in London at the time.

Thus no more than two or three families and only about a dozen people were resident in Wooda Bay from 1841-81. Presumably the lord of the manor lived elsewhere most of the time. But Slattenslade was a busy farming community in the nineteenth century. There were four households and never less than fifteen people recorded at the time of the censuses and, in 1841, there were twenty-five souls living there.

The 1840 tithe map shows that West Woodabay Wood, then Slattenslade Wood, was divided into a number of strips running north-eastwards about twenty or thirty yards wide which were rented by twelve local farmers.

In 1841 there were two farmers, William Latham and Amos Sloley. Amos had seven children, all with marvellous biblical names — the boys had Old Testament names and the two daughters were called Mary and Dorcas. The two agricultural labourer householders were James Widden and Thomas Lord.

Ten years later William Latham, who employed an agricultural labourer and a servant, had the biggest farm of 56 acres and Amos Sloley farmed 48 acres. His son Joshua was a carpenter-journeyman. James Widden was still an agricultural labourer, but sadly Thomas Lord had become a widower and a pauper agricultural labourer. However, Thomas had his brother and son living with him to help support him. They were both agricultural workers.

1861 recorded Moses Sloley as the principal farmer with 60 acres and employing a carter and a house servant. Thomas Ridd was the other farmer with a servant and a visitor, farming 40 acres at the time of the census. James Widden was listed a retired farmer. Benjamin Lock, pensioner (Royal Marines, Greenwich), was the fourth householder and he and his wife, Ann, had an interesting boarder with them, Annie Betsy Ridley, aged 2.

Moses Sloley had increased his land still further in 1871, farming 80 acres and employing one labourer and one male farm servant (indoor). Benjamin Lock and James Widden were still present but James (whose family is the only one to appear in all five censuses) had become a labourer again at 78 and his son, James, was a tailor. The name Crang was present for the first time. Richard Crang farmed 50 acres and had Samuel Sloley for his servant (also indoors, like Farmer Sloley's).

At the time of the census of 1881 George Norman was the foremost farmer. He had a farm of 60 acres and employed one boy and one servant. Richard Crang still had 50 acres. We see the first Slattenslade woman landowner in forty years in the person of Margaret Widden, widow of James. Her son, James, was with her still working as a tailor. Benjamin Lock, pensioner, continued living at Slattenslade.[1]

Two distinguished visitors rented the main residence at Wooda Bay in the 1880s. Edward Warne of Eton came with a party of 17 'counting horses, his mother and her maid, two babes and six servants'. Baroness Marie de Tanlegues wrote in 1889 that 'she wasn't really responsible for the damage to the yacht but that she would pay if it was insisted on'.[3]

In the 1890s two daughters of Richard Crang, Minnie Jane and probably Bessie Mary, worked at the Manor, as Wooda Bay house had come to be known. In 1895 the Manor, owned by Colonel Lake, was being run as the Wooda Bay Hotel. Richard Chaldon Crang was in charge from 1895-1900. Apparently, he farmed at the manor house as well as taking guests. In the Register of Parliamentary Electors of Martinhoe for 1901 Richard's son, Herbert John, was listed as the occupier of the Wooda Bay Hotel.[4]

The population figures in Martinhoe from 1800 more than doubled to 335 by 1831. By 1891 they had dropped to 165 equalling the number recorded in 1801, the lowest in the nineteenth century. Up until the Second World War the numbers were under 200, reaching their maximum in the twentieth century in 1921 when there were 220 souls in the parish. The lowest figures for nearly two hundred years were recorded in 1971 when there were only 120 people living in Martinhoe. In 1981 the local population had risen to 155.

Nineteenth century directories record that there were just over 2,500 acres of land in the parish, with 73 acres of foreshore. Half the parish was common or moorland in 1890, and in 1900 this open land was reduced to one-third until after World War II when it became almost negligible.[1]

Official spellings for Woody Bay have varied. As has already been noted, in an eighteenth century lease it was called 'Whiddiby' and a contract of 1823 referred to 'Weddebay'. The parish registers of the early nineteenth century termed the bay 'Withy Bay'. The census returns for 1841 and 1851 both used the title 'Woodybay'. 1861 and 1871 used 'Woodabay' and 1881 reverted to 'Woodybay'.

In some newspaper correspondence to the *North Devon Journal-Herald* between 1895 and 1897, writers argued whether the name Woody Bay should revert to Woodabay as it is shown on the Ordnance Survey map of 1809. Thomas Wainwright of the North Devon Athenaeum argued for the latter. The Reverend R. W. Oldham of Martinhoe suggested that the Bay should be called Weddebay as this was an older spelling than Woodabay. Another correspondent agreed the name should be Weda or Wedaby, as pronounced by the locals. Apparently, Wainwright's view prevailed — for a while.[5]

When Benjamin Greene Lake of the Priory, Orpington, bought Martinhoe manor from Sir Nicholas William Throckmorton in 1885, he mortgaged the lands for £25,000 to settle a debt he had incurred by speculating in Kent coal shares. He was an adventurous schemer (articled as a solicitor in 1861), careless with other people's money. He mortgaged one property to finance developments and to pay for another, and offset losses by borrowing further money. He also misappropriated trust funds (of which he was a trustee) and his clients' money. Lake blamed his cousin, George Edward Lake (who died in 1899), for causing their firm Lake, Beaumont and Lake, to mount up debts and for not disclosing them.

In October 1900 the London Bankruptcy Court revealed that Benjamin Lake was over £200,000 in debt. Outwardly respected, Lake was, at the time of his trial in January 1901, chairman of the Law Society and a Devon JP and because of this, the *North Devon Journal-Herald*'s report of the case said that his 'failure caused a great sensation'. He maintained that he was unaware of the losses of his firm over the years but, nevertheless, he was found guilty on most counts. Colonel Lake was sentenced to twelve years in prison; as one wag put it, he received one year for each of the houses in the Bay. He died in 1909, presumably on remission, at his son's home (ironically, in Wandsworth).[6,7]

After Colonel Lake's 'heavy failure' his estates, the Wooda Bay estate and the rest of Martinhoe manor, termed the 'Sporting Agricultural Estate', together approaching 2,000 acres, were to be auctioned in 1900. The Wooda Bay Station Hotel (Moorlands) which had been built by Lake, Hunter's Inn, a number of local farms, other property and various plots of land in and around Wooda Bay and Martinhoe were included in the sale. The sale catalogue stated that the Wooda Bay estate (Lots 1-9, about 150 acres) stood 'unrivalled' in its varied scenery, its water supply and drainage, its soil, its climate and hygiene and that is was 'ripe for further development, either as a popular Pleasure Resort or for the erection of high-class Residences'. The catalogue, never lacking in superlatives, proclaimed that the estate 'possesses a marvellous combination of Woodland, Cliff, Seascape and Moorland Scenery including some of the finest views in the West of England', and that 'The remainder of the Property forms a unique Sporting Estate' (some 1,775 acres).

Martinhoe Town Farm was termed the 'Reputed Manor of Martinhoe', which had the gift of advowson and the lordship of the manor. Mr G. W. F. Brown of Barnstaple acquired it, apparently on behalf of Mr Charles Frederick Bailey JP of Lee Abbey. Squire Bailey bought the first nine lots of the Wooda Bay estate, which included the manor house (then the Wooda Bay Hotel), for £6,500. He also bought Ranscombe which comprised a small holding of 86 acres, including a stone house occupied by Mr James Bond, near Woolhanger, for £500. The brochure stated that the Reverend R. W. Oldham held the living of St Martin, Martinhoe, together with the rectory and glebe land since 1886. Myrtle Villa was owned by Mr W. Keeling on a 99-year lease from 1892. His combined rents were £29.10s. and his land made up two rods. 'The well-known Wooda Bay Golf Links' were included in lot 10 of the sale comprising Slattenslade Farm and surrounding lands.[8]

There was no mention of other houses at Slattenslade in the Wooda Bay sale brochure apart from the Farm House. Presumably they had fallen into disrepair or the vendor did not wish to mention them for some reason. Apparently, Frank Norman, son of George, recorded in the 1881 census, bought Kittitoe near Heddon's Mouth at the sale in 1900; and possibly the Mr Whiddon who bought some accommodation lands, including part of Woolhanger Common and probably the Station Hotel, may have been James Widden, the tailor, formerly of Slattenslade. Benjamin Lock had probably died by 1900 and it seems that Annie Lock, his widow, continued to live on, undisturbed, in what was known as Annie's Cottage. This was on the same side of the road as the farmhouse by the large new barn. The hovel, as it probably was, is now reduced to a heap of stones mournfully intermingling with ivy, brambles, snowdrops and some old hardware. At any rate, Richard Crang must have either leased or bought Slattenslade Farm House from C. F. Bailey.

Frances Amelia Moysey bought Myrtle Villa (which was once rather pretentiously called Myrtle Grange) at the beginning of the twentieth century so that she could overlook the Bristol Channel. Her husband, Lewis Moysey, who had been a ship's surgeon in the RAMC, was drowned when the *Glenart Castle* was torpedoed and sunk in 1918 only thirty miles from Lundy. Her housekeeper and gardener were Mary Louise (Louie) and William Frederick (Bill) Marlow.

There is a delightful brochure of Woody Bay Hotel (formerly the Glen Hotel) *c.* 1935. The writer, E. P. Leigh-Bennett, extols the delights of travelling there by the Lynton & Barnstaple railway: 'the toy train, taking the traveller through scenery the like of which for extreme loveliness is unique in all England'. If travelling by car, the writer begs that the visitors get out of the vehicle above the hotel on the moorland overlooking the sea, the cliffs and the wood. From the latter the hotel peeps 'a little Swiss-like chalet'. Leigh-Bennett praises the rooms and the plain, homely local fare served in the dining-room.

He suggests that bathing, fishing and walking are the chief pastimes from the hotel. Like others before him, he is ecstatic about the walk to Highveer. There is a wonderful photo of two flappers, one in a cloche hat, seated on the cliff path, enjoying the view. 'I know that there is no more beautiful and tranquil spot on all England's coast lines,' says Leigh-Bennett. The hotel's terms were three guineas a week in the spring and four guineas at Easter and in the summer.[9]

Richard Berry of the post office was the proprietor of some refreshment rooms in 1921, and in 1931 Thomas Henry Ridd owned 'refreshment rooms' on Inkerman Way.[10]

In an historical newspaper article written in 1938 in the *North Devon Journal-Herald*, W.J.H. says that in 1630 Risdon was the first to write that Martinhoe was the home of Martyn (of Tiron, Normandy). The property and land passed through various well-known local names, including the St Albins (or St Albyns who held the seat until 1422), St Maugers, Thomas Barry, Philip Percival, George Courtney and the Throckmortons. In 1850 C. F. Bailey of Ley Abbey owned the rest of Martinhoe and Croscombe manor. The nineteenth century Martinhoe rectors were John Dovell (1789), Joseph Dovell (1840), Charles Scriven (1857), William Gordon (1882) and Reginald Walter Oldham (1886-1927). The writer, W.J.H., ends by calling the district 'a veritable paradise'.[11,12] Since Sir Robert Throckmorton lived in Woody Bay in the mid-nineteenth century several of the manor owners have been considered eccentric.

A major bone of contention between successive owners of the manor house and other locals and visitors was the free right of way, or otherwise, for the public going to and from the beach. It was apparently Mr Stanley George Robert Holman of the Queen's Hotel, Cheltenham, who lived in the Bay during the years 1925-39, who started the 'Woody Bay Wars' with contenders for rights of way along the roads to the beach. He built a gate and a wall across the main route down to Woody Bay in an effort to exclude motorists, and in June 1939 Mr Holman appeared at the Exeter Assizes charged with and convicted for obstructing a footpath. Witnesses claimed that there had been complete access to Woodabay since 1870; certainly Colonel Lake had encouraged people to come to the Bay. Stanley Holman also tried to claim the Wooda Bay estate foreshore for himself.[13,14]

At a public inquiry by Mr Hugh Park QC, on behalf of the Devon County Council in September 1961 at Martinhoe, it was stated that Mr Smith, the owner of Martinhoe Manor at the time, had erected gates at the top of his roads barring public entry. In this and subsequent hearings it was alleged with some triumph that members of the sturdy Devon race had uprooted such gates and tossed some of them over the cliffs. At the inquiry locals insisted on their rights of way to the beach. Harry Richard Latham of Lorna Doone Farm, Parracombe, said he had been down 'for fishing or picking laver.' The reply given by the QC leading the inquiry, typical of those learned in the law but not necessarily in local natural history, was, "What on earth is that?" "Seaweed," (of course) explained Mr Latham. "It isn't everyone who likes it."

Robert A. Ralph, a 74-year-old taxi proprietor of Lynton, said he drove a pony and governess cart through Woody Bay in 1899. He said he remembered royalty there and that 'two princes drove through and up to Lynton station to go away'. William Henry Delbridge of Riverside, Barbrook, said that in 1899 he had hauled timber along the Woody Bay roads. In 1897 there had been a pub at the manor house.

But William Frederick Marlow of Myrtle Villa was a witness for Mr Smith, saying that he had known the estate for forty years and that there had been three gates there during Mr Holman's time, 'one above Ringapeak, another at the entrance to the woods and another on the road to Lynton'.

Mr Smith alleged that he had walls and fences and notices damaged by motorists visiting the Bay. He also said the roads were breaking up and that he had already spent over £2,000 on them.

In 1962 Mr Smith's solicitors, Furze, Sanders and Frith of South Molton, maintained that they would keep the gate padlocked at the top of the main route down to the beach until the Devon County Council would take over and maintain the Woody Bay estate roads. But the Devon County Council sought a road closure order for the beach lane although promising to put a car-park at the top.

People wrote to the papers, principally the *North Devon Journal-Herald* and the *Western Morning News*, pleading for the continuance of old public rights of way. But Mrs Marlow of Myrtle Cottage wrote saying she did not wish, as a ratepayer, to support the Devon County Council in the upkeep of the road past her cottage for the benefit of those 'Automobile Automatons' too lazy to walk!

Barnstaple Rural District Council and most local folk continued to oppose the Devon County Council's plans to close the Woody Bay beach road to traffic. Mr Hugh Park QC, for the Devon County Council, in a 49-page report published in April 1962, had concluded that the public did have vehicular rights over the Woody Bay roads because they had had rights of passage over them from 1890-1919. The merits of a new car-park continued to be argued about. Despite Mr Park's findings the road still had a locked gate at the top. Mr John Dallyn of Martinhoe was reported saying in July 1963 that he and ninety per cent of the locals felt so strongly about it, they had written to the Devon County Council.

Before he died in September 1963 Mr Smith had tried to get planning permission for a shop and refreshment kiosk at Martinhoe Manor for his tenants and the visitors — rather against the tenor of his attempts to bar vehicular traffic, it would seem.

Mr Dawe, Mr Smith's South Molton solicitor, at an April 1964 meeting, said he put up the original iron gate to stop the 'vilification' and 'victimization' of the Smiths. Objectors to the road closure included Mrs Sylvia Mary Putley of the Woody Bay Hotel, Mrs Dora Cartwright-Williams of Little Raveley, Dr and Mrs Roger West of Woody Bay Cottage, Miss Abrahams of Wringapeak, G. E. Smyth of Martinhoe, Miss D. E. Blackmore of Caffyns Cross, the Lynton and Lynmouth Publicity Committee, the Exmoor Resorts Publicity Committee, the Lee Abbey fellowship, and the Exmoor Society (the Exmoor National Park having sided with the Devon County Council). Mr Latham of Parracombe said the Devon County Council should take over the upkeep of the road and provide a car-park. In July 1964 Mr S. A. Bailey, for the Ministry of Transport, confirmed that the Devon County Council's case held no water and that Mr Park's inquiry three years before showed that the public had vehicular rights there.

The beleaguered and puzzled Smiths believed that the visiting public were intruding on their demesne and were trying to defend the latter. Mrs Smith refused to remove the offending barring gate unless her rights of property *vis-à-vis* the roadway were confirmed. By November Mrs Smith had been forced to remove the gates. But she would not co-operate with the Devon County Council over building a car-park in Woody Bay. The Ministry of Transport ruling that the road should stay open led Mrs Smith to sell much of her land, and the road, to the National Trust. Thus in 1965 the National Trust bought 120 acres of the Woody Bay estate, thereby ensuring its protection and upkeep (subject to voluntary contributions) for unborn generations. What a splendid conclusion to the vexed questions and bitter relations which folk had argued about and indulged in, respectively, over the rights of way in the Bay for so many years![15,16]

In April 1978 *Devon Life* carried an article about Woody Bay and Martinhoe Manor (then comprising 26 acres) which suggested that in King Henry VIII's reign deer hunting took place there. There is then a great leap in history to the infamous Colonel Benjamin Lake (not Wade as written here) in the 1880s. Jan Corlett, the vivacious owner written about in the article, wanted the Manor to have a dual purpose — to serve as holiday flats and as a Field Studies and Activities Centre with the aid of COSIRA. Apparently, the centre never got off the ground although there are many natural resources close at hand. Jan, like so many of the other residents in Woody Bay, could think of nowhere more like 'Paradise'.[17]

When Mrs Moysey died in 1944 she left Myrtle Villa to Mrs Marlow. Thereafter, Louie Marlow and her husband worked at Lee Abbey and for people in Woody Bay at various times. She worked for Jill Cartwright-Williams who said that nothing frightened Louie, except tree branches which whipped off her hat as she returned home along Sir Robert's path in the dusk. Mrs Marlow was a good-hearted, busy little woman and she cooked excellent cakes on a number of paraffin stoves. Mr Marlow kept bees and grew vegetables in his steep garden.

They never had a car and must have been extremely fit, as Mrs Marlow walked the two or three miles over the common on the top of Woody Bay to Martinhoe Cross to catch a bus to Lynton or Barnstaple to do her shopping, and then walked back with her baskets full. The couple, who lived at Myrtle Villa for 50 years, died in the late 1960s within a few days of each other, both aged over eighty. They had three sons apparently, the second and third being John and Pat. The latter married Olive Charlton the sister of Jack and Bobby. The eldest son was brought up by an aunt and not much is known about him outside the family.[18]

Three houses in Woody Bay are let as holiday cottages or flats today. There are also two hotels — the Woody Bay Hotel and the Red House, where the Scotts and the Gardners, respectively, give the visitor a warm welcome. Locals frequent the Woody Bay Hotel bar and the lunch-time bar meals are delicious and very reasonable. The home-made soup is as good as may be found anywhere. Martinhoe Manor (the Wooda Bay Hotel from the mid-1890s until 1912) now has self-contained holiday flats. The present owners, Gordon and Barbara McKay, bought the Manor 'to preserve it in its natural and peaceful state for all to enjoy'. The old nearby farm buildings comprise a private residence called Hawks Hill Cottage. Slattenslade Farm used to advertise 'Morning Coffee' in the 1970s but does so no longer. It is now solely a private house which is the home of Robin and Valerie May, and a group of its farm outbuildings was sold for conversion in October 1988.

References to Chapter Two

1. Martinhoe parish registers. Estate books and Land surveys concerned with Martinhoe. Marriage settlements of George Throckmorton and Anna Maria Paston. Various leases. Land Tax assessments. Tithe Survey 1840. Sale indentures and maps. Census returns. Electoral rolls. Kelly's *Directories of Devon* various. All the above are in the North Devon Record Office.
2. *Some Notes on the History of Martinhoe from the Earliest Times*, Revd Reginald Walter Oldham (1886-1927).
3. From research of the Sanford family undertaken by Donald E. Bennett, partly based on *Notes on the History of Nynehead Court*, Ruth Whittaker (1979).
4. *Murray's Handbook for Devon* (1895).
5. *North Devon Journal-Herald* (16 October 1895-21 July 1897).
6. Death Certificate: Benjamin Greene Lake, 22 June 1909.
7. *North Devon Journal-Herald:* 'The Affairs of B. G. Lake of Martinhoe', (1.11.1900) and 'The Prosecution of B. G. Lake' (24.1.1901).
8. *The Wooda Bay Estate, North Devon, near Lynton Particulars, with Plans and Views* (1900) Messrs. Walton & Lee, Auctioneers and Surveyors, 10 Mount Street, Grosvenor Square, London W.
9. *Woody Bay Hotel* Brochure (*c.* 1935) E. P. Leigh-Bennett Copyright: Arthur Morgan Edwards, Woody Bay Hotel, North Devon.
10. *Directory of Devon* Kelly (1930 and 1939).
11. *Directory and Gazetteer of the County of Devon* M. Billing (1857).
12. *North Devon-Journal Herald* (22 July 1938) 'Our North Devon Parishes W.J.H.'
13. *Express and Echo* (2.12.33, 13.1.34) and *Western Morning News* (9.12.33).
14. *Along the South West Way* A. G. Collings (1985) Tabb House.
15. *North Devon Journal-Herald* and *Western Morning News*(29 September 1961-11 March 1965).
16. Ministry of Transport letter to The County of Devon (24 July 1964).
17. *Devon Life* (April 1978) '. . . round and about the rural development of the rural north.'
18. Dora Cartwright-Williams, Little Raveley, Woody Bay (1970s).

1939 —

THE MOST BEAUTIFUL SPOT IN THE WEST.
Remote from Aircraft.
Hot and Cold water in all bed rooms.
Every modern comfort.
Specially reduced terms for long stay.
A.A. & R.A.C. H.R.A.
Particulars from Resident Proprietor.
E. HOGAN,
WOODY BAY HOTEL,
PARRACOMBE, N. DEVON.

Woody Bay Hotel
and
MARTINHOE MANOR.

Woody Bay showing Martinhoe Manor in foreground and Woody Bay Hotel, 600 ft. above sea level.

"What a heavenly place this is!"

Remote from the stress and strain of modern times, inaccessible to heavy traffic. The Hotel is fully licensed and the keynote is good value.

Tel. Parracombe 64.

Terms on request from the Resident Proprietors

Mr. & Mrs. J. C. PUTLEY,
Woody Bay Hotel, Parracombe, N. Devon.

1950

Early advertisements

BERRY'S
Post Office,
Woody Bay
(3½ miles from Lynton).

Are noted for their Real Devonshire Cream Teas and Light Luncheons. Board Residence.

o o

Visitors from Lynton please take the Inkerman Bridge Road, by Letter Box; if from Martinhoe Common, follow telegraph wires towards Sea.

WOODY BAY. Apartments or Board. Splendid position, nearest Sea. Modern house, indoor sanitation. Mrs. BERRY, "Woodcot" (The Post Office), Woody Bay, Parracombe, Devon.

"Trees"

Woody Bay, Parracombe, N. Devon.

Book early for a delightful holiday in North Devon.
Five minutes from sea through woodlands.
Beautiful scenery. :: Excellent Cuisine.
From 6 gns. each. Special terms Spring and Autumn.

Proprietress. *Tel. Parracombe 87*

THE HALT, Caffyns, Lynton

BOARD RESIDENCE or BED AND BREAKFAST.

Fully Modern, embodying the comforts of a West End Hotel. Wireless. Electric Light. Bath (H. & C.). 2 minutes from Train, 'Bus and Lynton Golf Links. 940 feet above the Sea, affording glorious views of Sea & Country.

AFTERNOON TEAS.
LIGHT LUNCHEONS.

Inclusive Terms 2½ Guineas per Week.

Proprietor: S. A. ARDISS ("Stanley"), late of Lee Abbey Hotel).

CAFFYN'S FARM
CAFFYN - LYNTON

Adjoining Golf Links and overlooking Lee Bay with views of Welsh Coast. Own farm produce and poultry. All modern conveniences. Electric light, bath (h. and c.). Terms moderate.

Proprietress: Mrs. K. E. Pugsley.
Telephone:— Lynton 114.

CHAPTER THREE

MARTINHOE'S ANCIENT PEOPLE; THE ROMANS; THE NORMANS; MEDIEVAL TIMES; ST MARTIN'S CHURCH AND THE LOCAL CHURCH TODAY

The Stone Age people built a henge (circular monument of wood or stones) near Woolhanger Wood. Other earthworks near by may well have been made by them.[1] In Neolithic times there were 'knapping floors' (or flint 'factories') at Woody Bay Cross.[2] The Greenwell Barrows at Martinhoe are the work of Bronze Age folk, lying near the upper Woody Bay car-park. These are probably burial places and date from *c.* 2000-1300 BC. Several of these tumuli were opened by the Revd J. F. Chanter in 1906 but he found nothing of great interest.[3] Near the parish boundary between Martinhoe and Parracombe is the Iron Age Beacon Castle which displaced the work of an earlier people. It is a raised round earthwork probably dating from the second or third century BC.

The Reverend R. W. Oldham, who was rector of Martinhoe from 1886-1927 and an amateur local historian, knew that there were mounds on the magnificent Beacon site above the Cow and Calf, but he did not know that they were once part of a Roman camp. The Romans built a signal station there in *c.* AD 58-60 where 70 or 80 soldiers were garrisoned until *c.* AD 75. Their main duty was to keep watch for the warring Silures of South Wales. There is a twin fortlet to Martinhoe (800 feet) in Old Barrow, County Gate (1,100 feet). Both forts had 'a circular outer enclosure about 300 feet in diameter with an outer ditch, and with an entrance on the south (landward) side'. There was a 'square inner enclosure with its entrance on its north (seaward) side'. Each fort had a beacon with which to signal to the other. 'The site was abandoned when the Silures were finally subjugated.'[1-4]

Lady Fox and Dr W. Ravenhill excavated the Roman site at Martinhoe from 1960-1. Their findings showed 'the foundations of two blocks of barrack buildings, remains of clay ovens and a small furnace and fires in the inner enclosure'. It probably held up to 80 soldiers under a centurion. The excavators discovered foundations of wooden huts in the inner enclosure, which was 90 square feet with two ramparts and ditches. It was entered from the north by a roughly paved causeway between the ends of the ditches. 'There was a beacon cairn for signal fires, between the two ramparts near the north-eastern corner.' Pottery, including Samian ware, coins and weapons were also found. These discoveries can be seen in the Museum of North Devon, Barnstaple. Martinhoe Fortlet and Old Barrow (or Burrow), Countisbury were built not only to withstand the Silures from South Wales, led by Caratacus, but also their potential allies, the Dumnonii of North Devon.[4,5,6]

In 1066, as mentioned in the Domesday Book, the manor of 'Matingeho' was given to Geoffrey de Mowbray, Bishop of Coutances, who gave it to a Norman soldier, Drogo. The Reverend Reginald Walter Oldham believed that Drogo granted it to another Norman soldier, Martin of Tiron in Normandy. Martin called the church after his namesake, the saintly Bishop Martin of Tours of the fourth century. However, the name Matingehoe means the hill of Matta's people and the village is not named after Martin.

The church of St Martin's in Martinhoe is an attractive stone building with a slate roof. The Revd R. W. Oldham thought that a church would have stood here in William the Conqueror's time when the manor of Martinhoe was in the possession of the Bishop of Coutances. He reckoned the simple original church of cob and thatch would have been built 500 years before that. The present church was built in approximately 1300 and the oldest parts are the tower of primitive style (which is very similar to that of the eleventh century St Petrock's Church, Parracombe); the chancel, which shows Early English features such as the windows with their trefoil arches and flat segmental window arches; and the south-west corner of the nave. The tower has a low opening into the church and narrow slit windows and was probably a hiding place in turbulent times.

There was a dedication or rededication of St Martin's in 1338 by the Bishop of Waterford. In 1868 there was a similar event conducted by Bishop Temple when Mr Scriven was rector and James Dovell and Moses Sloley were churchwardens. The fifteenth century screen was demolished at some period and replaced at the time of the Victorian restoration when the musicians' gallery, medieval oak benches with carved ends, and the eighteenth century box pews were removed. The north aisle was built in 1868 amongst other additions. A new vestry was built in 1851 and was once used as a day school. (Sir William Throckmorton built the village school in 1872.) To support Mr Oldham's theory that there was an earlier church before 1300 is the existence of the plain, circular Saxon/Norman font, formerly in St Martin's but which now stands in St Petrock's Parracombe. The present ornate font in St Martin's was made by a Barnstaple mason, Pulsford, in 1864.

There still remains the Elizabethan communion table which has been well preserved, partly because it was covered with whitewash for forty years. There are two very old bells, mentioned in the inventory of 1553 made by the Royal Commissioners, inscribed Maria and Sancta Maria. The larger one was probably made in the mid-fourteenth century and the smaller, in the early sixteenth century. The chalice (1640) is said to have been fashioned with silver from the Combe Martin mines. The accompanying paten was made in 1684. The church also possesses a decorated silver cream jug, dated 1873, which is inscribed, 'Rev. J. Hannington to F. Dovell', together with a child's spoon and fork. Presumably, the one-time curate, James Hannington, was godfather to Florence Dovell of Killington.

The list of rectors dates definitely back to 1270 and before that to one du Pyn (date unknown). There was a John Martyne, echoing the name of his church, instituted in 1517. Miss Oldham writes that 'in Parson Joe Dovell's time everyone came to church, except Mrs Rottenbury of Cherryford who was afraid of catching cold if she cleaned herself'. When Joe Dovell was rector of Martinhoe 'there were raised seats by the tower end, in which the musicians sat. Old Bill Crang's father played the bass viol, and another old man, the clarinet.'

The fame of at least one of the nineteenth century clergy spread beyond the immediate locality. The Reverend Charles Scriven is largely known today for having had James Hannington for his curate. Hannington wrote that the people at the Rectory thought him 'very eccentric' which was true of a number of West Country clergymen in the nineteenth century. Hannington's biographer, E. C. Dawson, related Mr Scriven's views concerning his curate's cliff-climbing exploits: 'Good Mr Scriven did not half like these perilous freaks.' The rector called James and his companions, who included his son George, 'pups' and said they were 'like moths buzzing round a candle'. The curate named the largest cave they found 'Cave Scriven'. Hannington was much loved by the locals and it was while he was at Martinhoe that he found 'peace with God through our Lord Jesus Christ' and came into 'full assurance of faith' which led him to become a bishop and journey towards his martyrdom in Africa in 1885.

Mr Oldham had a seating plan for the church in his unpublished *History of Martinhoe*. The first four pews were occupied by Woody Bay, Lee Abbey, 'Crosscombe' and Killington which, equating Woody Bay with Martinhoe as it encompassed the main residence (Martinhoe Manor), befitted the four main manors of the area. Behind them were placed Slattenslade (situated on the southern heights of Woody Bay) and the Mannacott and Kemacott groups. Mr Oldham recorded that there were villages of Slattenslade, Martinhoe Town, Milltown and Kimacott Cowton. The probably Saxon Slatynslade (Slattenslade) was first mentioned in writing in 1544. It would have been (like Martinhoe, Killington, Croscombe Barton, Kemacott, Kittitoe, Ranscombe and Mannacott) an early medieval settlement consisting of several small and remote farms, forming a practically self-sufficient tiny hamlet in a valley.

Old surnames in the parish registers, dating from 1632 onwards and still recurring locally today, are Blackmore, Pile, Berry, Lord, Dallyn and Crang. The population of Martinhoe and Trentishoe parishes in Mr Scriven's day did 'not much exceed three hundred souls'.

There are memorials to Margaret Blackmore (d.1683), daughter of Hugh Wichehalse, the first of his family to own Ley Farmhouse (Lee

Abbey), and several later Blackmores who were related to Richard, the novelist.[1,3,5,7,8,9] There are a number of old graves commemorating members of the Ridd family, whose name was immortalized in *Lorna Doone*, and many others belonging to old families in the churchyard.

The entry in the burial register for 3 April 1787 reads, 'A stranger drowned [this word is crossed out and 'found' is substituted for it] on the shore at Heddon's Mouth, Whose name is unknown, was buried December 6th, 1787.'

There are a number of melancholic or morbid inscriptions on the graves at Martinhoe. Two Walter Frys buried next to each other have almost identical verses on their headstones. That of the senior Walter who died in 1803 aged 47 reads:

Think with yourself as you pass by
As you are now so once was I
As I am now so you must be
Prepare for death and follow me

However, there are also some very uplifting and comforting words of scripture on lots of other graves which redress the balance. The following is written at least twice:

(The eternal God is thy refuge, and)
Underneath are the everlasting arms

William and Ann Latham of Slattenslade who both died in the 1870s have inscribed on their joint headstone:

My flesh and my heart faileth
but God is the strength of my heart
And my portion for ever

Susan and Lillian Latham who died in the 1890s have engraved on their stone this proclamation of triumph:

With Christ which is far better

John Delbridge lived at Woody Bay Cottage, I believe, as a lime-burner until he became the tenant of William Keeling at Myrtle Cottage in 1892. He returned to the beach cottage in 1903 when Mr Keeling came to live at Woody Bay permanently. He died in 1906 aged 85. He was the son of Bartholomew who was the first person to appear on the censuses residing at Woody Bay in 1841. The grave of John Delbridge and his wife, Joanna, contains also the remains of their sons, John, aged three, and Frederick, aged eight, who predeceased them. For all these reasons, the Delbridge family engage my especial sympathy.

One Martinhoe headstone says simply that William Auchingloss (1869-1900) 'died at Woody Bay', where he was presumably a visitor.

The donator of a farewell wreath to the Lynton & Barnstaple Railway when it closed in 1935, Captain Thomas Alfred Woolf OBE of the White House, was buried in St Martin's churchyard in 1937 aged 55 and his mother, Gertrude Mary, in 1936 aged 85.

The Richard graves are in Martinhoe churchyard. Dorothy Edith died in 1948 and her husband, Edwin Verney, in 1960. His mother-in-law, Margaret Vye Joyner, wife of Robert Batson Joyner CIE, died in 1942. They all lived at the Red House.

John Peak Crang of Seaview (Wringapeak) was buried in 1952 aged 84. Other Woody Bay dwellers more recently buried in the churchyard are Dora Cartwright-Williams' first husband, Group Captain Francis Cartwright-Williams OBE, RAF of Little Raveley, in 1956; and a co-owner of Martinhoe Manor in the late seventies, Mr William Albert Box, who died in 1986.

The Rectory is an attractive white Georgian house, built in 1800 and enlarged in 1843 and 1847. W.J.H., writing in the *North Devon Journal-Herald* in 1938, says that the Rectory in the time of the Reverend Charles Scriven was 'a neat and commodious residence'.[10] The Rectory garden is lovely. It has some magnificent and unusual plants, one of which is monkey musk, and a number of delightful features, such as a tiny maze, with a sundial in its centre. There are waterfalls and a small lake, where the Oldham children and grandchildren used to venture in miniature boats long ago.[11,12] In the grounds of the Rectory stands Hollowbrook Cottage which was probably a medieval church house.[1] The Rectory was on the market for £400,000 in 1988.

There is a 'Rhyme of St Martin's Church' which well expresses the faith of Christians down the ages worshipping in the tenacious wind-beaten church which stands on the heights of Martinhoe. It runs as follows:

> Hard by the Roman sentry kept
> His seaward watch for Celtic horde,
> While fitful Devon sunlight gleamed
> On heathen spear and pagan sword.
>
> And here through Devon mist and rain
> Came godly Christian men unknown,
> To build a Church in Martinhoe,
> To adze the beam and hew the stone.

Small trace the Roman left behind;
But grey St Martin's looks to sea,
Proclaiming on the wind's wild breath
The strong Faith of the Trinity.

So may she stand to speak the word
(To those who sail and those who plough)
That Christ who died upon the Cross
Is Lord in highest heaven now.

Long let her stones, with mystic tongue,
Tell out to mortals yet unborn
That deepest gloom of Calvary
Must yield to light of Easter Morn.
Alexander Hunter, Rector of Martinhoe, 1963

Today, instead of being coupled with Trentishoe as it was in the first half of the twentieth century, Martinhoe is one of a group of seven churches. The Lyn churches comprise Lynton, Lynmouth, Parracombe, Martinhoe, Barbrook, Brendon and Countisbury. Woody Bay, being part of Martinhoe, is included in this group.

At the end of November 1988 came a letter from Gordon Coates of Little Raveley, Woody Bay and a churchwarden of Martinhoe, to the parishioners. He gave the unwelcome but too often heard message that St Martin's was threatened with closure unless considerably more active support was forthcoming. It must have been with gratification and considerable relief that the present church officers found their meeting on 15 January 1989, which was called to discuss the future of Martinhoe church, so well attended by locals giving offers of help. Since then the church offices have been more fairly shared. But more congregational and hefty financial support is necessary to help keep the church alive.

From West Woody Bay one can see Lee Abbey, stalwart and strong, enfolded in the hills. Ley was recorded in the Domesday Book and was owned by Forde Abbey, a Somerset monastery, in the twelfth century. With the onslaught of the plague Hugh Wichehalse, a Barnstaple merchant, retreated to the large farmhouse at Ley Bay, the Ley Manor of *Lorna Doone*. Charles Bailey bought the estate in 1841 and rebuilt it (*c.* 1850)to make it look like an old abbey. In 1921 his son C. F. Bailey, known as 'Old Squire Bailey', who had inherited Lee Abbey and bought the Wooda Bay Building Estate, died. Lee Abbey was an hotel until 1939 when a boys' preparatory school bought it as a refuge at the outbreak of war. It was sold again in 1945.

In 1946 a small group of Christians bought Lee Abbey with a vision to use it as a centre from which to offer holidays where the Gospel could be preached and the faith and outreach of the guests enriched and renewed. They bought the 350-acre estate for £28,000 which had been raised through faith. Today the Community is a flourishing group of seventy people who work for very little remuneration though their faces express their inner reward. John and Gay Perry were the last Warden and wife and they guided the fellowship with gentle love. In the early part of 1989 John was instituted Bishop of Southampton. The Perrys' welcome and worthy successors are Mike and Frances Edson. Some 7,000 guests stay at Lee Abbey each year.[13]

The life of the Lee Abbey Community also spreads a considerable influence over that of Woody Bay. For not only does Lee Abbey practise Christian outreach far and wide but it also opens its heart and home to the immediate locals, not least the residents of Woody Bay. There is a women's Bible Study for those living in the neighbourhood who are interested. There are Open Days and Christmas or New Year parties, much enjoyed by Woody Bayites, amongst others, when the young Community members perform memorable music, and there is folk-dancing and an abundance of good food. Short epilogues proclaiming the Gospel on these occasions are refreshingly straightforward and thought-provoking. In 1979, when the snow was deep and the winter hard, Lee Abbey provided much needed Good Samaritan-like help by bringing their milk in tractors to those otherwise cut off from the outside world in Woody Bay.

References to Chapter Three

1. *Lynton and its Coast: a local history* Dr E. T. Mold, unpublished.
2. *Exmoor* S. H. Burton (1970) Hodder and Stoughton.
3. *The Parish Church of Saint Martin* Martinhoe Church leaflet, C.W.
4. *Exmoor's Archaeology: Early Man* L. V. Grinsell (1982) Exmoor National Park.
The Archeology of Exmoor L. V. Grinsell (1970) David & Charles.
5. *Churches and Chapels of Exmoor* N. V. Allen (1974) Exmoor Press.
6. 'Roman Excavations in North Devon throw new light on the Conquest' (1971) Local newspaper.
7. *Some Notes on the History of Martinhoe From the Earliest Times* 1st & 2nd Editions, R. W. Oldham (Rector Martinhoe 1886-1927), unpublished.
8. *Notes* (on Martinhoe) Marjorie S. Oldham (1889-1973).
9. *James Hannington First Bishop of Eastern Equatorial Africa. A History of His Life and Work* 1847-1885 E. C. Dawson. (1887) Seeley & Co.
10. *North Devon Journal-Herald* 'Our North Devon Parishes' W.J.H. (No.22 July 22nd 1938).
11. *The Old Rectory Martinhoe* brochure, Tony Pring.
12. Photograph album, R. W. Oldham.
13. *The Lee Abbey Story* Jack C. Winslow (1956) Lutterworth and various Lee Abbey brochures.

General

Devon Bridget Cherry and Nikolaus Pevsner (1989) Penguin Books.

Woody Bay, print c. 1840

Looking west c. 1880

Looking east c. 1890

West Woody Bay c. 1905

Looking east, photo with superimposed yachts and topmost house, early 1900s

Bathing Pool c. 1900

Stags on Manor Lawn, 1990: George Hepworth

Ladies' Changing Hut (bottom left) and Woody Bay Hotel c. *1900*

Woody Bay Hotel (from brochure) c. *1935*

Post Office c. *1900*

Coast Road c. *1895*

Coach Road c. *1895*

Wooda Bay Hotel (Martinhoe Manor) c. *1899*

Glen Hotel new road 1896

June 2nd 1898

Pier c. 1897, John Loveless Photographer, Lynton

Woody Bay c. 1899, Tom Bartlett, Postcard Views of North Devon, vol. 1, Badger Books

Woody Bay Pier c. 1900

11th June 1902

Workmen with steam winch 1896

Pier c. 1896, John Loveless Photographer, Lynton

Woody Bay Pier workmen, 1897

Pier c. 1897, John Loveless Photographer, Lynton

Woody Bay Pier 28th February 1896

Pier 13th June 1896

Woody Bay Pier 13th June 1896

Workmen and diver 1896

Hanging Water Fall, 1989

Bronze Age Barrows above Woody Bay (Martinhoe Church tower in background) 1990

The Beacon from Martinhoe

Top of Roman fort, Beacon Hill, Martinhoe 1990

Ridge of Roman fort looking towards Martinhoe 1990

St Martin's and Church house from the S.W. 1895

Road alongside Martinhoe Church 18th April 1907

Martinhoe Church with Martinhoe Town Farm (centre background) c. 1900

Martinhoe Church 9th August 1902, with Revd R. W. Oldham (centre)

Repairing St Martin's Church tower 1914

Elizabethan Communion Table, St Martin's

Martinhoe School (centre background) c. *1900*

Martinhoe School July 1894. The young rector, Reginald Oldham, and his wife Susan Conway on the left

Martinhoe School 25th May 1897

July 1912

Monsieur Fry, the Malet's tutor, at Martinhoe School November 6th 1901

Martinhoe Rectory February 1897

Martinhoe Rectory garden September 1902

September 1905, Marjorie Susan Oldham (right)

Slattenslade compound 1990

Slattenslade Farm and outbuildings 1990

Old farm buildings, Slattenslade 1990

Woody Bay beach party, 12th September 1907. Revd R. W. Oldham and his wife Susan (seated on left)

Scriven Cave
July 1899

Driving towards Woody Bay c. 1900

Old Caffyn's Golf Club House, Lynton Links 1970s

West Woody Bay from Crock beach, winter 1989

'German' collecting water at Woody Bay

Shelley lived here for 9 weeks in 1812, writing Queen Mab

Trentishoe Church June 1900

The Musicians' Gallery, 1990

Woody Bay Station c. 1900

Woody Bay Station early 1900s

Bob Jones

The author, Mark, Rachel and Deborah with Bob off Woody Bay, 1980

Outovercott June 7th 1900

Army Camp, Caffyns

Frank Hobbs

Horace Crang

Wooda Bay Golf Links, Foundations of hut 1990

Elkie Brooks, 1990

CHAPTER FOUR

WRITINGS ABOUT WOODY BAY, EXMOOR, AND NORTH DEVON

The earliest writers were not very complimentary about untamed Exmoor. In 1540 Leland wrote, 'Exmoor has always been the wild and desolate waste we now see.' Again, 'From Exford to Simonsbath Bridge a four miles al by Forest, baren and morisch ground, where is store and breeding of young Catelle, but little or no Corne or Habitation.'[1]

In 1597 John Gerard wrote of 'Devon, a solitarie place it is, the more commodious for staggs who keep possession of it.'[2] Defoe (1661-1731) supported Camden's view of Exmoor that it was 'a filthy barren ground'. He preferred 'lower . . . Devonshire . . . populous and fruitful'.[3] (Woody Bay comprises both the wild and the cultivated — high moorlands, forest, the wide expanse of sea below and fields and gardens.)

The moorland situation seems to have improved, at least as far as the inhabitants were concerned, by 1800. Richard Warner, writing of his walk through North Devon in that year, says, 'The peasantry of North Devon . . . are a very superior race . . . imbibing from the pure air of their native mountains mental vigour as well as corporal strength, they exhibit a sagacity and quickness'. 'The young Danmonii' possess 'colloquial civility' too. 'They have imbibed their manners from freemen.' [4]

George Tugwell, a delightful mid-nineteenth century writer, describes Woody Bay in his book *North Devon Scenery* of 1863 as 'a steep hill . . . embowered in the soft shadow of green foliage, catching from time to time delicious glimpses beneath the overhanging branches of the blue sea so far below. This is Woodabay. The path winds through the woods, nestles in the woods and finally emerges far above the woods on a windy down.'[5]

In his *Tourist's Guide to North Devon* of 1883 R. N. Worth is lyrical about Woody Bay. 'This is emphatically a place to be seen. The trees grow thick and tall almost from the very verge of the water and tower in slopes and terraces up the enclosing hills to the height of nearly 900 feet. Like every true Devonshire combe, Woody Bay has its streamlet here dashing and plashing over its rocky bed far down in the foliaged depths. A zigzag road on the bare hill-side of the Bay leads up to a bald, bleak common.'[6]

Unfortunately, these places are not as open a hundred years later. Bushes and scrub obscure the viewpoints of much of the landscape. However, since 1987 Steve Mulberry, the capable and caring National Trust Warden for Woody Bay, has engaged in 'operation rhododendron' to clear the woods as far as possible of the most effective ponticum variety, shader of light and thus destroyer of other fauna and flora. This clearance, apart from protecting other species, has opened up the woods and cleared spaces under the trees and between them.

J. L. W. Page, the famous topographer and writer of Exmoor in 1895, also praises Woody Bay as a sylvan combe — 'Woodabay beautifully timbered'. In his *Coasts of Devon and Lundy Island* (1895) Page calls Woody Bay 'a mere recess in the cliff at the base of a lofty semicircle of woodland'. He, like Worth, speaks of 'a sea of foliage covering the slopes almost to the water's edge'. He also makes the comment that 'above the woods a stretch of moorland rises another 300 feet against the sky'. He speaks disparagingly of the attempt at the time to elevate Woody Bay into a popular resort, even though there were only eight houses then. (Little Raveley was amongst four others not then built.) Worth is poetical about the Bay and Page likens its attributes to music. He writes, 'musical is the voice of the leaves stirred by the sea breeze, still more musical the song of the brook plunging down the glen to the stony shore below'.[7] (I think he might have added the changing tones of the sea to those of the woods and Hanging Water if he had lived here.)

Wooda Bay was once Whitabay according to Dulverton's Dr C. P. Collyns' *Chase of the Wild Red Deer* of 1902. Dr Collyns affirmed that the deadly hunting of deer took place in Woody Bay. In 1858 a hind from Sweet Tree Wood by Dunkery Beacon ran the length of the moors to Woody Bay (22 miles) with the hunt making the chase in 2 hours and 29 minutes, the record run of the season. But the woods could not hide the unfortunate deer and 'the hounds being close to her haunches, she leapt from the cliff (a height of about 300 feet) and was dashed to pieces. Old Warrior, one of the best hounds in the pack, shared her fate.' Apparently, there were only a handful of sportsmen including old John Beale, the huntsman, and the whipper-in at the finish.[8]

The Homeland Handbook of 1904 surpasses Worth in poetical description; it terms Woody Bay 'exquisite' — 'a semi-circular sweep of a trifle less than a mile in breadth, an almost unrivalled perfection of richly draped cliff and of rocky, barren hillside. The post office [now Trees], where a real Devon tea may be obtained, affords a beautiful view of the Bay.' (The latter had been obscured gradually since then, at least till the 1970s, but in the mid-1980s the owner of the Manor House and of Trees cut a passage through the woods by felling the oaks blocking the view.) 'It is now some years,' the guide continues, echoing Page, 'since attempts were made to develop this sylvan Paradise. One or two villas were built, and a pier was run out into the sea: whilst roads were lavishly engineered to render the place easier of access. The pier has disappeared, but the villas remain. There is a hotel at the bay [the Glen] and another [Moorland] at Woody Bay Station, two miles inland. Each extremity of the bay is guarded by a cliff of 500 or 600 feet in height, only the lower part of which is naked, undeniable rock. The rest is robed from top to bottom with masses of hanging oak —

A Sylvan scene; and, as the ranks ascend
Shade above shade, a woody theatre
Of stateliest view . . .'

The writer then speaks of the lower promontory of Wringapeak which 'is pierced by a natural arch'. He tells of the Inkerman Bridge (built in 1857 to commemorate the Crimean victory), which spans the Hanging Water as it streams through the wood beneath the hotel and emerges from the trees, falling almost vertically on to the main beach.[9]

Baring Gould is fairly prosaic as he begins to write about the Bay in his book *Devon* of 1907. For example, 'The walk along the coast to Wooda Bay ... is to be recommended.' Later he writes that it is 'a lovely scene of wood, rock and sea. The villas dotted about, red tiled, are picturesque.' But he adds the criticism, 'The disadvantage of the place is that the access to the beach for bathing is by a long and steep descent.'[10]

Today, local residents tend to be glad of this slight deterrent, for it means that, on the whole, only walkers, swimmers, fishermen and lovers of natural beauty bother to trek to Woody Bay.

C. G. Harper's classic, *The North Devon Coast* written in 1908, is the first topographical book to describe in some detail the landslip of Crock Point in 1796 and the Woody Bay speculation of the late nineteenth century. The landslip comprised a farmer's fields slipping into the sea because of landsprings and the digging of the clay for pottery to be sent to Holland. Harper tells us that Colonel Lake's timber pier was 'speedily washed away' by the sea. The writer also states his preference (like mine) for the name 'Wooda Bay' as opposed to 'Woody Bay'. He speaks of 'delightful lanes leading round the shores of the bay' and of the waterfalls. [11]

The 'verdure' of Woody Bay is extolled by W. Riddell, like writers before him, in Twiss & Sons' *Guide to Lynton and Lynmouth* of 1910. He, too, mentions the 'misty spray' of the waterfall. Interestingly, (agreeing with Dr Mold of Lynton today) Riddell affirms 'the best way to reach Woody Bay in fine weather is by boat from Lynmouth' spotting the notable places *en route* and 'the rare formation of the cliffs and the marvellous colouring of the rocks.'[12]

In *Coast Scenery of North Devon* (1911) the geologist, E. A. Newell Arber writes of the access to Woody Bay. He says 'several paths traverse the beautifully-wooded Hog's back cliffs ... From the shore, near the ruined [now restored] limekilns at the old pier, the coast may be explored some distance to the East towards Crock Point, but to the West progress along the rough [manor] shore is more limited.' Newell Arber reports the Woody Bay hog's-back cliffs are 900 feet high, and that the cliffs are composed of Hangman Grits and Lynton Slates. 'Its wooded slope is so steep that it is impossible to follow it in many places, where no path exists . . .' The Hanging Water tumbles '900 feet in less than half a mile' he writes, 'ending in a fine fall about 30 feet in height.' Newell Arber calls Woody Bay 'a wild and desolate moorland' and says the hog's-back cliffs can be studied to fine advantage here, probably better than anywhere else in Devon.[13]

C. S. Ward, writing in 1908 in the *North Devon and North Cornwall Guide*, says the road from Lynton to Heddon's Mouth via Woody Bay is 'among the choicest in the district'. He calls Woody Bay a 'steep and richly wooded glen'. He mentions the smattering of houses, but shrewdly says he does not think the speculator will make much of the proposed development as the shore (except at low water) is minimal and the place is 'too confined'. Ward writes of the Lynton & Barnstaple Railway and the Wooda Bay station and says it is 'somewhat remote' from the hamlet of the same name. He thinks the name Woody Bay 'was a guess by the Ordnance Survey'.[14]

John Presland in *Lynton and Lynmouth* (1918) says the 'sweep of the cliffs' at Woody Bay 'is bold and beautiful'. He is afraid of the crop of new building in the place lest it turn it into a popular resort. He says that from the high road the Bay resembles a toy town.[15]

Burrow's *Guide to North Devon and Cornwall* (1918) relates that Woody Bay was a favourite spot for excursions from Ilfracombe.[16]

Ward Lock's *Lynton and Lynmouth* guide of 1920-1 calls Woody Bay a charming glen with 'a lovely pine wood' walk or roadway. It speaks of university reading parties going there before the war relishing its 'quiet and retirement', and praises its attractive villas.[17]

Woody Bay is 'a glory of trees' and there is 'a very wonderful path leading Westwards to Woody Bay', so writes L. du Garde Peach in *Unknown Devon* (1927) and he speaks of the disembodied feeling when 'hanging between the vast emptiness of the sky above and the great shining expanse of the Channel below'.[18]

The Homeland *Lynton and Lynmouth* (vol.37) speaks of the fine views to be had from Woody Bay station of hills and sea and Wales beyond. It describes Woody Bay as 'an almost unrivalled perfection of richly draped cliff and of rocky barren hillside.'[19]

Will Sherracombe in *Devon Exmoor* talks about the Glen Hotel being 'built on the edge of a precipice half way down the hill.' He recalls the construction of the pier. 'I was staying at the hotel at the time and well do I remember the opening thereof. It was a real Devonshire day of continuous driving rain: the steamer arrived off the pier, but as this was not long enough was unable to come alongside, and two wretched pressmen were landed in a small boat. The venture was unlucky as most of the building was swept away in a fierce gale, while the remains were sold for scrap iron so that hardly any trace remains.'[20]

'More beautiful than Lee Bay is Wooda Bay beyond,' asserts J. H. Wade in his *Rambles in Devon* of 1930, 'where the sea laves the foot of a wooded and exquisitely tinted amphitheatre.'[21]

S. P. B. Mais, writing in *Glorious Devon* (1932) says of Woody Bay, 'It is a tiny forest covering the whole of one wide and lovely bay. As you drive along its shady road and marvel at its quietude you can see neither houses nor sands nor waterfalls, though all are there.'[22]

W. Harding Thompson and Geoffrey Clark in *The Devon Landscape* (1934) similarly write that 'the dense groves of Wooda Bay appear to rise from the sea itself'.[23]

Walking with Fancy (1943) describes country moods. The chapter 'Devon in August' is about birds, set against the beautiful backdrop of Woody Bay's western shore. The author is E. L. Grant Watson and the book has the distinction of being illustrated by C. F. Tunnicliffe. 'Devon in August' speaks of the promontory opposite the cliffs of Wringapeak which remind Watson of the landscapes of Chinese painters of the sixteenth and seventeenth centuries. From here he watches the razorbills and guillemots precariously raising their young on rock ledges. He also observes the gulls attacking the rock-pipits. Beneath the watcher are the 'rocks and the waves and the green swirl of the deep water'. He says that to him 'most wonderful, most fascinating of all is the sea, constantly swirling and advancing and receding at the base of the cliff.' He concludes there must be 'master-thought' behind it.[24]

F. C. Elliott writes about Wooda Bay in his *Exmoor* of 1947. He mentions that 'Lee Abbey has now become a rest home for the Church of England Clergy.' (Far from it, the visitor observes, as he notes the pain-staking and hard work lavished on the guests and estate by the Community all the year round.) Elliott imparts the interesting information that Philip Oppenheim once lived at Martinhoe Manor. Could he be connected with the author E. Phillips Oppenheim who wrote one of the very enjoyable novels about the Bay? Elliott suggests it will be hard for the visitor 'to tear himself from this elysium.' Unlike some of the other writers Elliott felt 'the cottages and farms seemed to have merged themselves into nature's back-ground; they might have grown up with the trees themselves.'[25]

Surely S. H. Burton has written the definitive present-day topographical work on *The North Devon Coast* (1953). His books would inspire the most timid to tramp the North Devon Coast Path. He writes of 'the arboreal beauty of Woody Bay' and of the 'striking' Wringapeak promontory. Like other writers, Burton asserts that the Hanging Water 'in its brief vehemence closely resembles Coscombe Water at Glenthorne' further east along the coast. 'Indeed,' he writes, 'there can be no questioning the charm of this sequestered spot: the sea, the cliffs, the oak and ash bowers that hang right over the bracken and the heather,and the babbling call of the curlew count the lazy hours of a summer day in this green and quiet place.' Here Burton demonstrates his power not only of accurate and sensitive local description, but also to express this in compelling prose.

'From Woody Bay to Heddon's Mouth,' says Burton, 'is one of the finest cliff walks along this coast.' He refers to Arber as he writes, 'the

Woody Bay cliffs are among the most spectacular along the Severn Sea coast, nine hundred feet in places and heavily wooded with so steep a seaward slope it is impossible to walk along them.' He speaks of the well engineered Swiss-type roads and the spring of the Hanging Water rising 'on a moorish upland near Greenwell corner' not far from Woody Bay station.[26]

A *Lynton and Lynmouth* guide of 1959 gives further details of a landslip at Crock Meads, but dates it at 1814 (perhaps there were two major eruptions). A Farmer Bromham rented Leemouth Farm and this particular slide occurred while he and his family were in church at Martinhoe. His fellow parishioners turned out to help him save his ricks. 'A great deal of corn was lost spread over nine acres, but no livestock. For weeks thousands of tons of clay were spread along the beach at low water mark . . . of all colours.' More lumps of differing coloured clay have been spotted by locals as late as the 1880s (and on into the twentieth century) after further landslides.[27]

Miss M. S. Oldham (1889-1973, daughter of the Martinhoe rector, R. W. Oldham) writes a similar account of the 1814 landslip. She adds there was a crack of eighty yards long by two yards wide within twenty yards of the house. Also, that with the clay, remains of ancient timber props could be seen, believed by her to be Roman. She says George Crocombe, born in 1798, told these details to Mr Bailey of Lee Abbey.[28]

In *Ships and Harbours of Exmoor* (1970) by Grahame Farr the author discusses the development of Woody Bay by Colonel Lake. In the Order he obtained in 1889 to enable him to build the pier, Lake properly, and with some irony, was called the 'Undertaker'. As well as the pier Lake started to build the Old Harbour Inn in 1895. [29]

The official *Exmoor National Park* booklet of 1974 (editor J. Coleman-Cooke) speaks of the heavily forested Woody Bay slopes and mentions the sea-bird colony at Wringapeak, including fulmar petrel nests. It adds, 'it is dangerous to try and descend the cliff face.'[30]

In the excellent *South-west Peninsula Coastal Path* guide (1980), by Ken Ward and John H. N. Mason, there is a map opposite each page of description. It was published just in time for the eventful six-day North Devon Coast Path walk of that year, undertaken by myself, my son Mark aged sixteen, and his sister Rachel, a tenacious twelve-year-old. Messrs Ward and Mason speak of the 'thick woods' of Woody Bay and of 'a fine grassy track along the cliff to Hunter's Inn . . . and another high cliff path with fine views from every angle'. The latter is the 'attractive' and 'exhilarating' 'mountain goat' route. The top path (the old coach road) runs through 'a grove of trees then out on the cliff with marvellous views wherever you look.'[31]

The Lords' photocopied booklet, *The Spirit of Exmoor* (1981), gives some fascinating and kaleidoscopic details of Woody Bay and its surrounds.

The Lords quote Jan Corlett, a mid-twentieth century owner of Martinhoe Manor, reporting that Hawks Hill Cottage used to be the home farm for the manor, complete with piggeries whose inmates had plenty of acorns to hand in the woods. The authors give the approximate map reference for the now largely obliterated Hannington's path as OS 180/SS 659 497 in between Highveer and Martinhoe beacon. (In fact, this reference is for the western path, but the Lords describe the eastern one running down to Clinnock Hole which is adjacent to St Hubert's Grotto which Archer called 'Big Cave' and is now known by local climbers as Hannington's Cave.) [32] These two tracks are shown on C. H. Archer's map of Woody Bay to Bosley Gut, based on an Ordnance Survey one which accompanies his climbing papers.[33]

The Exmoor National Park Authority's *Enjoying Exmoor* (1985) emphasizes 'the most dramatic section of coastline is that between the Valley of Rocks and Heddon's Mouth.' From Woody Bay to Heddon's Mouth there are guillemots, razorbills, kittiwakes, fulmars and jackdaws and ravens.[34]

Robin Richards probably has more right to relate stories of the Bay from the twenties onwards than most people today, since he lived at the Red House as a boy. In the spring edition of the *North Devon Magazine* of 1987 he wrote an article entitled 'Woody Bay And Before'.

He tells plummy tales of locals of his day, in particular of the feuding between the wrongly styled 'Lord of the Manor' of Martinhoe manor, Stanley Holman, and Judge Fraser of Crock Pits (now Pines). They fought over a field adjacent to Fraser's house, which Holman swore he owned. The Judge was apparently a terrible driver of his Armstrong-Siddeley car. He could not change gear smoothly, especially into first and ended up crashing into the wall at Stubb's Corner — by the coach road to Heddon's Mouth. Holman, in his efforts to deny local rights of way, put down concrete and two pieces of local railway line at the top of the coach road from the Red House to the beach. But local lads quickly removed the tracks and threw them over the cliff. However, later on nature put Holman's plan into action by producing a landslip over the roadway, turning it into a path.[35]

Probably it would have been Mrs Marlow, the housekeeper (and future owner of the cottage), and not the lady of the house who cooked the home-made fare for the 'youths of Woody Bay'. Frances Amelia Noble had married Lewis Moysey RAMC in 1901. Lewis, Doctor and Captain, was serving in the *Glenart Castle* when she sank. 'Mamie' believed that her husband might one day swim back to her. This was a vague possibility as he might have been stunned or rendered unconscious and washed ashore. Frances, like Queen Victoria with Prince Albert's clothes, reverently had all Lewis's naval uniform hanging in the hall waiting. But Mrs Moysey's hopes must have receded with time.

In his article 'Woody Bay Pier' for *An Anthology of North Devon* (1983),

Richards mentions that after the pier was removed (1902) Stanley Holman of the Manor and Dr Woodhouse of Woody Bay Cottage competed for lobsters on the pier base in the thirties.[36]

So the circle is completed with the later writers, like the earliest ones, extolling the glory of Woody Bay — with its rich and hardy oaks tumbling steeply to meet the deep sea. There has been woodland on Exmoor since the Ice Age tundra disappeared 12,000 years ago.[37] What Burton said has always been the case since prehistory: 'Woody Bay lives up to its name.' Several travelling friends visiting me and looking out of my windows have said, "You must have one of the best views in the world." It is almost impossible to describe the haunting beauty and grandeur of Woody Bay adequately.

References to Chapter Four

1. *Itinerary* (1534-1543) John Leland (pub. 1710).
2. *The Herball* John Gerard (1633) and 1636 Edition of Thomas Johnson.
3. *From London to Land's End* Daniel Defoe (1724).
4. *A Walk through Some of the Western Counties of England* Revd Richard Warner (1800) ptd. by R. Cruttwell.
5. *The North-Devon Scenery-Book* George Tugwell (1863) Simpkin, Marshall & Co.
6. *Tourist's Guide to North Devon and The Exmoor District* R. N. Worth (1883) Edward Stanford.
7. *An Exploration of Exmoor* John Lloyd Warden Page (1895) Seeley & Co., Ltd.
The Coasts of Devon and Lundy Island John Lloyd Warden Page (1895) Horace Cox.
8. *Chase of the Wild Red Deer in the Counties of Devon and Somerset* Charles Palk Collyns (1902) Lawrence & Bullen Ltd.
9. *Lynton, Lynmouth & the Lorna Doone Country* W. Riddell (1904) The Homeland Association Ltd.
10. *Devon* S. Baring Gould (1907) Methuen & Co., Ltd.
11. *The North Devon Coast* C. G. Harper (1908) Chapman & Hall Ltd.
12. *Guide to Lynton & Lynmouth* W. Riddell (1910) Twiss & Sons.
13. *The Coast Scenery of North Devon* E. A. Newell Arber (1911) Kingsmead Reprints (1969).
14. *North Devon and North Cornwall Guide* C. S. Ward (*c.* 1908) Thomas Nelson & Sons.
15. *Lynton and Lynmouth* John Presland (1918) Chatto & Windus.
16. *Burrow's Guide to Devon and Cornwall* 1918-, J. Burrow & Co., Ltd.
17. *Lynton, Lynmouth & Exmoor* —, 1920-1, Ward Lock & Co., Ltd.
18. *Unknown Devon* L. du Garde Peach (1927) John Lane, The Bodley Head Ltd.
19. *Lynton & Lynmouth, c.* 1925, The Homeland Association Ltd. Vol.37.
20. *Devon Exmoor* Will Sherracombe (1928) Heath Cranton Ltd.
21. *Rambles in Devon* J. H. Wade (1930) Methuen & Co.
22. *Glorious Devon* S. P. B. Mais (1932) GWR Co.
23. *The Devon Landscape* W. Harding Thompson & Geoffrey Clark (1934) A. C. Black Ltd.
24. *Walking with Fancy* E. L. Grant Watson (1943) Country Life Ltd.
25. *Exmoor* F. C. Elliott (1947) The Saint Catherine Press Ltd.
26. *The North Devon Coast* S. H. Burton (1953) Werner Laurie.
27. *Lynton & Lynmouth* 1959 pub. Reginald T. Reeves.
28. Notebook M. S. Oldham (first quarter of the 20th century).
29. *Ships and Harbours of Exmoor* Grahame Farr (1970) Exmoor Press.
30. *Exmoor National Park* ed. J. Coleman-Cooke (1974) His Majesty's Stationery Office.
31. *The South-west Peninsula Coastal Path* Ken Ward and John H. N. Mason (1980) Charles Letts & Co., Ltd.
32. *The Spirit of Exmoor* N. E. & R. V. Lord (1981) Norman E. Lord.
33. *Coastal Climbs in North Devon* C. H. Archer (February 1959) — unpublished — map of Woody Bay to Bosley Gut.
34. *Enjoying Exmoor* ed. Leonard Curtis (1985) Exmoor National Park Authority.
35. *The North Devon Magazine* 'Woody Bay and Before', Robin Richards (Spring 1987) Badger Books.
36. *An Anthology for North Devon* ed. Rosemary Anne Lauder 'Woody Bay Pier' Robin Richards (1983) Badger Books.
37. *The Trees and Woods of Exmoor* Roger Miles (1972) The Exmoor Press.

CHAPTER FIVE

BRIGANDRY, SMUGGLING, SHIPWRECKS, GHOSTS, FOLKLORE, WARTIME HAPPENINGS AND STRANGE NOISES

It is believed that the Doones, who had settled on Exmoor, held sway there for most of the seventeenth century as they plundered, robbed and murdered in and around the moorland farms. The notorious robber clan, immortalized by R. D. Blackmore in his novel *Lorna Doone* (1869), are supposed to have come from Scotland and have settled in the Doone Valley (probably Lank Combe) near Badgworthy Water not far from Malmsmead and Oare. Born a Scottish nobleman, Sir Ensor Doone apparently was driven from his country by a cousin and from thence he travelled to the West Country with his family and retainers. There they intermarried with the locals and, disdaining poverty, formed a cruel band of thieves.[1]

On one of their forays Carver Doone (Ensor's son) and a small band attacked a farm in the parish of Martinhoe, tenanted by Christopher and Margery Badcock. The latter was alone in the house with her baby and her maid, while her husband still worked, ploughing in the fine February dusk. Carver made off with 'the healthy and upright young woman, with a good rich colour', while the maid hid. The followers left behind, annoyed at the lack of any real or rich spoil on the farm, made sport with the baby, throwing him up and down, finally letting him crash to his death on the lime-ash floor. As they did so they mercilessly rhymed,

> If any man asketh who killed thee
> Say 'twas the Doones of Bagworthy.

When Blackmore used this macabre story in *Lorna Doone* his editor put as a footnote, 'The following story is strictly true.'[2] L. B. Thornycroft wrote, 'this is reputed to be the incident which finally decided the entire countryside to rise against the robbers and attack their stronghold.'[3]

In her notebook Marjorie Oldham, daughter of the Reverend R. W. Oldham, wrote about various curious matters in Martinhoe especially of the nineteenth century. Her piece entitled 'the Last Case of Sheep Stealing in Martinhoe 1827' is quoted verbatim:

> 'John Geen and his sons Hugh and George, all of Martinhoe, were seen by Richard Jones (then 20 years old) pushing a sheep down the cliffs at Wringapeak. He then saw them go down and cut it up. They beckoned to him to come down, but he refused. He heard afterwards that they had meant to kill him if he had, to prevent him telling of them. Chaldon Crang was the owner of the sheep; he had lost many this way. George Geen, who was half-

witted, turned King's Evidence, and both his father and brother were arrested and hung.'[4]

The Richard Jones involved was the one of whom Hannington wrote 'when Richard was a boy he had been the best hand in the Parish at climbing the "cleve".' Later, Jones helped Hannington and his friends cut the latter's daring and acclaimed paths down the Martinhoe cliffs.[5]

There must be more accounts of smuggling in Woody Bay than I can unearth. However, here are two such incidents. The first is undated. An exciseman chased a smuggler from the Valley of Rocks to a dangerous gorge heading the Woody Bay cliffs, close to the edge of the road. The exciseman caught up with the smuggler here and, gripped in their death lock, they both fell over the edge.[6] (These cliffs make a dramatic backcloth to a murder such as the fictitious one described in Malcolm Elwin's *The Little Hangman.*)

The second occurrence, involving a ship (the story of which is to be found in a document in the Bideford Maritime Museum), deserves to be quoted in full. 'In 1804, suspicious of cargo being landed near a limekiln, the revenue cruiser, "Shark", sent a boat ashore at Woody Bay. The 50 ton ship, "Margaretta of Bideford" had landed 219 kegs of brandy, 150 of gin, 9 of wine, together with 693 bags of salt, 8 bales of tobacco and a bag of pepper. This was seized and the "Margaretta" condemned to be sold.'[7]

Miss Oldham related that Mrs Patt of Martinhoe told her of a tall old man in a long coat who used to call, masquerading as a rag-and-bone man. In reality he sold smuggled spirits. Cottagers could have them at a reduced price if they threw in a good dinner. Mrs Berry told Miss Oldham that once there were three coastguards at Martinhoe Town, one an Irishman, with his family in Ireland, lodged for years with Farmer Ridd. Another lived in a cottage which was later burnt down, with his wife a 'bedlier', the whole family living in her bedroom.[4]

The diary of Martinhoe's renowned nineteenth century curate, James Hannington, recorded that Carpenter Richards of Martinhoe (possibly the Richards who ran Hunter's Inn) had been imprisoned for smuggling. His last words were, "I love Mr Hannington." James, characteristically, wished that it had been 'the Lord Jesus' whom Richards had loved at the last.[5]

An exciting tale of a fleeing soldier is that of Major Nathaniel Wade during Monmouth's Rebellion of 1685 (against James II). The troops landed at Lyme Regis with Venner, a relative of the Lynton Wichehalses, in command of Wade's Company. There was a skirmish. Venner was wounded and Wade took command. Major Wade fought at Sedgemoor but because of danger he withdrew to Ilfracombe. (Other soldiers fled to Watchet or Minehead.) At Ilfracombe Nathaniel Wade commandeered a boat. He recorded that fifty people were on board. Two frigates were in the vicinity and the vessel was embayed and ran ashore near Lynmouth —

either at Woody Bay or Sillery Sands in all probability. The soldiers dispersed. Major Wade hid in the woods at Hillsford Bridge. He was picked up by a local girl and taken to Farley Water Farm. From there he went on to a Cheriton farm (then Brendon Rectory) and Brendon church where the vicar spotted him. Another version has John Wichehalse, his servant John Bab, and some other men capturing Wade. Amazingly, the latter was set free and ended his life in Bristol. Another story is told of a Monmouth rebel escaping to Bonhill Wood.[3, 8]

Sillery Sands is a more likely landing-place for Wade, looking at the sequence of events on the map, but since this book is primarily about Woody Bay, romantically I like to think Colonel Wade might have come ashore here. Certainly, if a fugitive had gone to Bonhill he might well have landed at Woody Bay.

Another shipwreck took place near the site of the Wooda Bay pier. In 1895, when employees of Messrs Dixon Bros. of Swansea were engaged in laying the first piles of the new pier at Woody Bay, a heavy gale struck the barque *Canada*. A few days later 'huge pieces of wreckage were seen floating [in the water and littered] about the beach'.[9]

Riddell was the first writer to term an intriguing ghost story, the *Legend of Woody Bay*. The Squire of Woody Bay 'many years ago' who was a drunkard and a gambler and thus a near pauper, determined to rob one of his tenants of twice his rent. However, the farmer concerned apprehended and shot the owner of the manor upon his arrival at the farm. The Squire's ghost haunted his tenant's farm where 'nothing prospered'. One parson of Trentishoe did not suffice to lay the ghost who would not leave the place until six parsons undertook this task. The Squire was told not to return until he could 'draw a truss of sand with a rope of sand to the top of High Veer Point', which of course could never be accomplished, and the ghost gives 'howls of rage and despair . . . as the sand falls again to the beach.'[10]

There are three other more specific versions of the story, two of which are told by A. G. Collings in a later and most entertaining and informative book. He first relates that Sir Robert Throckmorton, the owner of much land in the immediate locality, constructed a lower road to the manor house known as Sir Robert's Path.

Collings quotes George Tugwell, saying that (for his misdeeds) Sir Robert Chichester of Croscombe Barton was condemned to haunt the base of a sheer cliff on the shore. He was to make a rope of sand to pull his carriage up the cliff face and then along Sir Robert's Road. Locals in the mid-nineteenth century reckoned they heard his angry voice as he worked away. Again, they believed they saw him on the common with his hounds who had fiery tails lightening the night.

Collings pours scorn on the second version of the tale, about an old soldier returning from the wars and seeking shelter at Croscombe Barton. In the night he apprehended and shot the much hated Sir Robert Chichester, leader of a band of robbers. Buried in Croscombe churchyard he would haunt and terrify the locals. Parson Brinkworthy caught him at Woody Bay and condemned him to bind the pebbles into faggots and tie them up with ropes of sand and roll them up the cliff. As they fell back he would give vent to loud unearthly cries. But there is no Croscombe churchyard, Sir Robert was buried at Pilton and there was no local Parson Brinkworthy.[11]

Squire Bailey of Lee Abbey told Marjorie Oldham the following version of the story. Sir Robert Throckmorton, a landowner in and around Martinhoe, gambled away his money till he was penniless. He decided to steal from his well-to-do farmer tenants. He planned to rob a rich one living at Bon Hill. However, he was caught and shot by the farmer with a blunderbuss. Thereafter, because Sir Robert haunted the farm, the animals died. The efforts of the Martinhoe parson to exorcise the ghost were of no avail. So the farmer asked six priests to come and perform the exorcism and this had the desired effect. They set the spirit the task of making ropes of sand on the beach between Woody Bay (main beach) and Crock beach, below the great red cliff. If he could haul himself up with these ropes he would be freed. Miss Oldham wrote that locals still reckoned that 'on wild and stormy nights' Sir Robert could be heard in full cry above the cliffs.[4]

Once a coach fell over the cliffs apparently between Pines and the White House. More recently another sad accident resulted in a car going over there. This stretch of road is an eerie one.

There is a tale of a headless horseman who has been seen up on the moorish ground above Woody Bay or on Sir Robert's Path, but I have not met anyone who has been confronted with this ghost.

Two of the Manor guests have recently sighted, individually and on two separate occasions, a grey figure apparently coming through the wall below Woody Bay Cottage. The holidaymakers both enquired whether there had been a door or a gate in the wall at one time.

Other present-day locals say that they feel a peculiar chill going along Sir Robert's Path towards Inkerman Bridge.

On 3 October 1989 at 9 p.m. two young women in their twenties, who were staying at the Manor, walked up Sir Robert's Path towards the hotel with their brothers strolling behind them. The two groups became separated with the girls, walking and talking animatedly, going ahead. They suddenly felt taps on their shoulders and spun round simultaneously, intending to reprimand their brothers for startling them. The boys were not there but, instead, a smallish figure in a cloak and hood was darting and dancing behind them. As for his face, they could only see his square white lower jaw. The girls' brothers some way back had not seen a thing.

The terrified young women ran up to the hotel where Mrs Scott was able to pacify them a little. But they returned still shaken to the Manor. The girls also said that they had found some steps off Sir Robert's Path apparently going to nowhere through the woods (in fact, they are part of a track made by Colonel Lake which ran to the hotel). The next day the women went to Barnstaple Library to do some research as to whom the figure might have been who had frightened them so much. They wondered if something terrible had happened there in the past at the hour and date when they had seen it. They read that Sir Robert Chichester had been a fellow for going after the ladies so thought they had seen his ghost. But if this apparition had been associated with the name Sir Robert at all, then surely it should have represented Sir Robert Throckmorton, the Martinhoe manor owner to whom Woody Bay belonged in the mid-nineteenth century and who made the path along which the girls walked.

The last two Manor house owners report that there is a friendly ghost at the Manor and that their dogs would not go into a particular room for some strange reason.

The Valley of Rocks (Stones in the old days) beyond Woody Bay to the east and towards Lynton is a series of amazing piles and shapes of jagged, pointed rocks, boulders and cliffs. It has its ancient stone circles and is the site of old legends and the seat of rich folklore.

E. A. Newell Arber believed that a stream ran through the Valley of Rocks and S. H. Burton names this the Lyn. The now dry valley was formed as it is, partly by aerial weathering and probably by Ice Age coastal streams which were blocked by ice and debris and thus ran parallel to the shore before finding an exit. The tops of some crags may have been decapitated by Wolstonian ice. Sea erosion has also played its part in shaping the valley and its cliffs.[12-17]

However, others say that a Black Abbot, alias the Devil, had a hand in re-forming the Valley of Rocks. It is related that the Valley was once the site of a castle dwelt in by the monk and Lady Edith Sigvald, who worshipped strange gods there around the year 500. When the abbot finally revealed himself as the devil and carried away Lady Edith into the darkness an earthquake swallowed up the castle destroying the evil therein.

In the nineteenth century a wise woman known as Mother Melldrum lived here. Her real name was Aggie Norman and she lived in a hut her husband built for her at the top of Castle Rock. She was the oracle whom John Ridd consulted in *Lorna Doone*. She died in 1860. It is alleged that both the forms of Lady Edith and Mother Melldrum are perpetuated in the White Lady whose shape is silhouetted between the huge rocks against the sky at the summit of Castle Rock.[18-21] Other tales claim that the rocks in the Valley are petrified men.

There is a sad legend about the fate of a beautiful heiress in nearby Lee Bay. It is fancied that in the sixteenth century Jennifried de Wichehalse of Lee Abbey, whose family have monuments to their name in Lynton and Martinhoe churches, was jilted by her betrothed. On hearing the news of his betrayal, the luckless Jennifried flung herself over the cliffs to her death at a spot now known as Jennifried's Leap. Her father Edward de Wichehalse is supposed to have fled to England from the persecuting Spaniards but there is no historical basis for the existence of Jennifried. However, Hugh de Wichehalse's great-grandaughter, Mary, did fall over the cliffs at Lee Bay in the eighteenth century.[3]

Marjorie Oldham recorded the story of the Reverend Joseph Dovell's brother, William, who lived at Middleton Farm, a family holding. He practised magic with a black book later burnt by the family. In Miss Oldham's day Mrs Patt lived at Martinhoe Mill. She said her father had an infallible cure for toothache. It was to bite one of the teeth from a dead girl with his own and drop the former on the floor.'Ever after his teeth ached no more.'

James Hannington wrote in his diary that old John Jones of Trentishoe could bless for the eyes and that he wanted to pass on this gift to the curate. Mrs Jones who lived near the parsonage had a seventh son who could bless for the King's evil. Hannington once tried a primitive form of faith-healing himself, which was nothing more than his ability to extract an unshakable trust from the patient in the spurious medicine he produced.[5]

The first aeroplane and German airmen to be captured in World War II landed on Martinhoe Common, Woody Bay on 22 July 1940. Jim Gammin, aged 47 and an ex-serviceman, was the first ARP Warden to capture German airmen in England. When the bomber crashed Jim left the cowsheds on the farm at Kemacott where he was working and ran to the spot. He helped the pilot and two of the crew to escape from the blazing plane. One German attempted to escape by parachute but was killed in the fall . . .[22]

Keith Howes of Croyde is the source of a most fascinating wartime story. It was passed on by the barman of Hunter's Inn. Two Germans who had been there in the war told it to him at the hotel. They had been in U-boats in the Bristol Channel. Evidently, each submarine was designated to a particular bay with fresh water along the North Devon coast from which to collect their water supply. The two Germans in question were in the U-boat which was to replenish its water supplies at Woody Bay. The vessel duly drew into the Bay at dusk. While it waited silently the men jumped into the water with their clothes on. The washing of clothes and men was conducted simultaneously and joyously, whatever the weather, by the men who experienced shortage of water otherwise; their normal conditions were oily, cramped and claustrophobic. The sailors would then row to the Hanging Water Fall to collect fresh spring water in containers. Thence they rowed back to the submarine which glided noiselessly away in the night. Apparently, locals and fishermen sometimes saw the German boat and sailors, but each side had a tacit agreement not to disturb the other's craft. Even policemen left them alone, as they realized they could never reach the next village on their bikes to raise the alarm before the submarine had gone.[23]

Lawrie Scott, a local hotelier, remarked that two ex-Wrens had visited the Woody Bay Hotel in 1988 and told him that they had observed U-boats here during the last war.

The Gardners related how when they first came to the Red House in 1978, they heard a strange hum when they went to bed at 11 or 12 in the evening. At that time the Woody Bay Hotel owners, Ron and Pauline Millet, had their deep-freeze outside the building. Eileen and Maurice thought the hum might emanate from there. They asked the Millets about the noise and the latter denied that it came from their freezer; they had heard the odd sound independently themselves and wondered what it was.

One night the Gardners and the Millets went up to the Coach House. They had a jolly evening and as they left in a spirit of hilarity, they were quietened by the most huge hum. It was very weird — almost as if they might be involved in some sort of space landing or encompassed by a happening from another world.

Next morning they taxed the Millets about the peculiar hum. The Millets thought that the spirit of the party might have affected their imaginations. Eileen said that, on the contrary, she drank very little because too much alcohol made her feel sick and as for Maurice, he had not been drinking at all for several months because of some medical condition.

However, neither the Millets nor the Gardners ever heard the hum again from that day on. Later, they understood that around that time questions were asked in Parliament about such a noise being heard along their stretch of coast. Was this why the enigmatic hum ceased? Was military equipment being tested at night-time making 'waves' causing noises to be heard in the vicinity, and did the government not wish the locals to know anything about this?

Eileen Gardner also told me that Bill Williams up at Little Raveley once showed her a newspaper cutting. This described how the Australian Parliament had been debating whether or not to allow Concorde to fly close to a major city, which Maurice thought was Melbourne. The contestant against this taking place cited an old lady from North Devon who lived close by the main path of some of the Concordes and she had been blown off her lavatory seat by the shaking that these aeroplanes caused. This lady was my roguish old friend, Jill (Dora) Cartwright-Williams.

References to Chapter Five

1. *Lorna Doone, Doone Valley* (1968) Sir Atholl Oakeley.
2. *Lorna Doone* R. D. Blackmore (1869/1873) Sampson Low, Marston & Co.
3. *The Story of the Doones* L. B. Thornycroft (1939) Barnicotts Ltd.
4. *Notes* on Martinhoe Marjorie S. Oldham (1889-1973).
5. *James Hannington: A History of His Life and Work* E. C. Dawson (1887) Seeley & Co.
6. *North Devon with West Somerset* No. 3 Beatrice and Gordon Home, The Homeland Association, Ltd. Frederick Warne & Co.
7. The Bideford Maritime Museum.
8. *Lynton and its Coast A Local History* — unpublished — Dr E. T. Mold.
9. *The North Devon Journal-Herald* (10 October 1895).
10. *Guide to Lynton and Lynmouth* William Riddell (*c.* 1900) Twiss & Son.
11. *Along the South West Way. Part 1: Minehead to Bude* A. G. Collings (1985) Tabb House.
12. *The Coast Scenery of North Devon* E. A. Newell Arber (1911 reprinted 1969) Kingsmead Reprints.
13. *The North Devon Coast* S. H. Burton (1953) Werner Laurie.
14. *Exmoor National Park* Ed. John Coleman-Cooke (1974) HMSO.
15. *No.6 Classic Landforms of the North Devon Coast* Peter Keene (1986) The Geographical Association.
16. *Along the Shore* Mike Towns (1984) Badger Books.
17. *Geology of the country around Ilfracombe and Barnstaple*, British Geological Survey, E. A. Edmonds, A. Whittaker and B. J. Williams (1985) HMSO.
18. *Legends of Devon* Sally Jones (1981) Bossiney Books.
19. *The Land of Lorna Doone* H. Snowden Ward Sampson Low, Marston & Co., Ltd.
20. *Who was Lorna Doone?* Barry Gardner (1989) Brendon Arts Limited.
21. *Lynton & Lynmouth* Lyn Valley Locals (1950s) Reginald T. Reeves.
22. Diary Frances Amelia Moysey *c.* 1918 onwards (Mrs Moysey died on 31 July 1944 in Lynton.)
23. Keith Howes, Croyde, 1988.

CHAPTER SIX

LOCAL ARTISTS AND ARTS

A number of authors, particularly topographical and historical ones describing the immediate locality, Exmoor and North Devon, have already been mentioned. There are a host of other artists of various kinds who have been here and whose work portrays the area particularly well.

The nineteenth century poets, especially the Romantic ones, fall into this category. 'Ever since Wordsworth and Coleridge walked the hills above Dunster to Lynmouth and the Valley of the Rocks, the natural beauty of West Somerset and North Devon has been recognized and praised.' So Noel Allen begins *The Exmoor Handbook and Gazetteer*.

In 1797 William and Dorothy Wordsworth rented Alfoxden House, Holford, Somerset. Here they had a number of literary friends to stay, and from this house the Wordsworths, Coleridge, Southey and the essayist William Hazlitt walked to Lynton. Engraved on slate above the doorway of the lodge at Watersmeet (built by the Reverend W. S. Halliday of Glenthorne in 1832) is a verse from a poem by Wordsworth:

> The spot was made for nature by herself;
> The travellers know it not, and 'twill remain
> Unknown to them; but it is beautiful;
> And if a man should plant his cottage near,
> Should sleep beneath the shelter of its trees,
> And blend its waters with his daily meal,
> He would so love it, that in his death hour
> Its image would survive among his thoughts

Coleridge was born in South Devon but said that the rest of Devon could not compare in grandeur and beauty with 'Quantock, Porlock, Culbone, Linton'. It was on one of his walks to Exmoor that he discussed with Wordsworth 'The Rime of the Ancient Mariner'. This has several West Country references. This is the Mariner returning to Watchet:

> O dream of joy! is this indeed
> The light-house top I see?
> Is this the hill? is this the kirk?
> Is this mine own countree?

The hermit might well have dwelt in the woods above Porlock Weir (or possibly at Minehead or even Lynmouth).

This Hermit good lives in that wood
Which slopes down to the sea.
How loudly his sweet voice he rears!
He loves to talk with marineres
That come from a far countree.
He kneels at morn, and noon, and eve —
He hath a cushion plump:
It is the moss that wholly hides
The rotted old oak-stump.

William Wordsworth wrote at least two lines of 'The Ancient Mariner' for his friend Samuel Taylor Coleridge. The two known lines are the following wonderful word portrait:

I fear thee, ancient Mariner!
I fear thy skinny hand!
And thou art long, and lank, and brown,
As is the ribb'd sea-sand.

Wordsworth's local poems were written mostly about Somerset. His best poetry was written after this period. Later he became Poet Laureate.

Robert Southey was Coleridge's brother-in-law and lived with his wife Edith (née Fricker) in Minehead. He was a Somerset man, a friend of Wordsworth's and also Poet Laureate. He wrote a sonnet while staying at the Ship Inn, Porlock, beginning:

Porlock thy verdant vale so fair to sight
Thy lofty hill which fern and gorse embrown
Thy waters that roll musically down,
The woody glens, the traveller with delight,
recalls to memory.

For a few weeks during July and August of 1812 Percy Bysshe Shelley lived in Lynmouth where he wrote part of 'Queen Mab'. His first wife, Harriet, described her West Country home in a letter:

We have taken the only cottage there was, which is most beautifully situated, commanding a fine view of the sea, with mountains at the side and behind us. Vegetation is more luxurious here than in any part of England. We have roses and myrtle creeping up the sides of the house, which is thatched at the top. It is such a little place that it seems more like a fairy scene than anything in reality. All the houses are built in the cottage style, and I suppose there are not more than thirty in all. We send to Barnstaple for everything, and our letters come but twice a week . . . It seems as if Nature had intended this place should be so romantic and shut out from all other intercourse with the neighbouring villages and towns.

Shelley, as well as being a fine poet, was the writer of 'A Declaration of Rights'. Some of these revolutionary leaflets he put into bottles which he cast into the sea. Others he had distributed in Barnstaple. Because of these activities Shelley was forced to leave Lynmouth. He is alleged to have escaped by boat to Wales via Ilfracombe to avoid arrest.[1-6]

Tennyson, the most famous nineteenth century Poet Laureate, also visited Lynton. He once wrote a stirring naval ballad called 'The Revenge', commending the Elizabethan North Devon sailors.

Some minor poets who wrote of North Devon and Exmoor include A. L. Salmon, T. E. Brown and Septimus G. Green.

These three poets wrote about Lynton and Lee Bay and so came to the immediate vicinity of Woody Bay for their inspiration. Writing at the turn of the century Salmon wrote 'The Mouth of the Lyn':

Forth from the fastness of its moorland home
With ceaseless din
Cometh the leaping Lyn,
Seeking the coast with constant fret and foam —
Bringing a wildness of the moors to wed
The wildness of the sea, — from ferny bed
And mossy boulders breaking, till it meet
The haven where its fleet
Disordered pulse shall stay its fitful beat,
And find a rest
In the more mighty swell of ocean's breast.[7]

T. E. Brown lived in Bristol in the latter half of the nineteenth century. He was a schoolmaster and taught rather unwillingly at Clifton College. He preferred to muse upon the Avon and Severn and take solitary walks upon the downs. He wrote a poem called 'Lynton to Porlock':

From Lynton when you drive to Porlock,
Just take old Tempus by the forelock —
In any case, don't hurry; time and tide —
Of course — I know. But, where the roads divide,
Upon the moor;
Be sure
To shun the via dextra,
And choose the marvellous ride
(One half-hour extra)

That zigzags to a gate
Nigh Porlock town — O, it is great,
That strip of Channel sea,
Backed with the prime of English Arcady!
It is not that the heather rushes
In mad tumultuous flushes
(Trickling's the word I'd use);
But O, the green and blues
And browns whereon the crimson dwells;
The buds, the bells;
The drop from arch to arch
Of pine and larch;
The scented glooms where soft sun-fainting culvers
Elude the eye,
And fox-gloves, like innumerous-celled revolvers
Shoot honey-tongued quintessence of July![8]

Septimus Green, like R. D. Blackmore for one of his stories *Frida; Or, The Lover's Leap*, takes the legend of Jennifried for a long poem set in Lee Bay (the next inlet eastwards from Woody Bay). Green wrote his 'Jennifred' in the 1890s and it was dedicated amongst other poems to Horatio Tennyson. The hapless Jennifried has been mentioned before. After being jilted by her fiancé, she is supposed to have thrown herself over the cliff beneath Duty Point tower in the grounds of Lee Abbey in the sixteenth century. Here is a description of the area from 'Jennifred' by Septimus Green:

Northwards in Devon, where the utmost verge
Of Exmoor's lone, inhospitable waste
Breaks into sylvan loveliness of combes,
Oak-clad, or fair with many a waving fern,
The red-deers' dewy haunts on summer eves;
Or opens suddenly into sounding bays,
Gloomily grand, or wooded to the wave;
Where the dark coast unto its neighbour coast,
Across the foam of Severn's silver Sea,
Smiles, sunlit, twixt the eclipse of cloud and cloud —
Here, clinging like a sea-bird to her crag,
Above the billowy surge, and overhung
With waving woods — spring's, autumn's
pride —
A virgin village, lovely Lynton, sits;
While at her feet, full fifty fathoms down,
Sweet Lynmouth, fairest of all ocean brides
Wild Neptune woos beneath our stormy steeps,

Sits, matron-like, in her meek privacy
Of shadow, from the busy world aloof,
With all her hamlet brood about her knee.[9]

One of the most renowned West Country writers of the nineteenth century was Charles Kingsley. He was a contemplative giant in the world of men and literature. He had a wide and deep mind that encompassed many subjects. But Charles Kingsley was no mere paper parson. He energetically championed the cause of the poor, practically in his own parish and by speaking forcefully for the Chartists in london, aiming to better the lot of the working classes generally: he was a Christian Socialist. He had lived in Clovelly as a boy when his father was vicar there. He felt deeply the loss of his fisher-boy friends who had drowned: these he never forgot. He wrote some verses about the cruel Clovelly sea called the 'Three Fishers'.

While he was recuperating at Bideford, Kingsley wrote the stirring sea story *Westward Ho!* needing to supplement his vicar's salary to support his family. He wrote *The Water Babies*, a children's tale, also encompassing the grand theme of the sea albeit in a very different mode from that embracing his rollicking romance of the Spanish Main.[10,11]

Charles Kingsley admired 'fair Lynmouth' so much that he said the village was 'unpaintable' with its 'chaos of rocks and mountain streams'. In his *Prose Idylls* he wrote a beautiful paragraph describing the coastline from Lynmouth to Heddon's Mouth (which includes Woody Bay) when he and a friend travelled on a Clovelly trawling skiff:

> What a sea-wall they are, those Exmoor hills! Sheer upward from the sea a thousand feet rise the downs; and as we slide and stagger lazily along before the dying breeze, through the deep water which never leaves the cliff, the eye ranges, almost dizzy up some five hundred feet of rock, dappled with every hue; from the intense dark of the tide-line, through the warm green and brown rock-shadows, out of which the horizontal cracks of the strata loom black, and the breeding gulls show like lingering snow-flakes; up to the middle cliff, where delicate gray fades into pink, pink into red, red into glowing purple; up to where the purple is streaked with glossy ivy wreaths, and black-green yews; up to where all the choir of colours vanishes abruptly on the mid-hill, to give place to one yellowish-gray sheet of upward down, sweeping aloft smooth and unbroken, except by a lonely stone, or knot of clambering sheep, and stopped by one great rounded waving line, sharp-cut against the brilliant blue. The sheep hang like white daisies upon the steep; and a solitary falcon rides, a speck in air, yet far below the crest of that tall hill. Now he sinks to the cliff edge and hangs quivering, supported, like a kite, by the pressure of his breast and long curved

wings, against the breeze.[12]

Kingsley's brother Henry wrote a compelling novel called *Ravenshoe* which is set in Trentishoe. Kingsley's daughter took the pen-name Lucas Malet and she was the authoress of a novel entitled *The Wages of Sin* which is a story about life in Clovelly.

Henry Williamson has been the West Country doyen of English literature to date in the twentieth century. He was a complex character who attracted unpopularity during the war for being a Nazi sympathizer. However, his sensitive and fine qualities came to the fore in rare insight into the nature of animals, which can be appreciated in his books such as *Tarka the Otter* and *Salar the Salmon* through his empathy with the country and the sea: he lived close to the moors at Shallowford and by the sea at Georgeham (which lies eastwards behind Croyde) and Ilfracombe.[13,6]

He wrote at least one local travel guide which contains a tiny pungent description of Woody Bay:

> We are now on the road once more, which went downhill and over a stream and uphill again leading through oak-woods and so downhill to the few houses of Wooda Bay, which also appeared to have been commercialised, and turned into an estate. Motor-cars were forbidden: good![14]

Sir Henry Newbolt, an eminent son of Devon spanning the nineteenth and twentieth centuries, first heard of the legend of Drake's drum while traversing Exmoor. Later he wrote a rousing ballad about it beginning:

> Drake he was a Devon man, an' ruled the Devon seas —

In a popular idiom Henry Newbolt wrote 'The Exmoor Hunting Song', which follows a route twenty to twenty-five miles across Exmoor traceable on the 1-inch OS tourist map from Bratton Fleming to Porlock (a course running inland behind Woody Bay).

> So hurry along, the stag's on foot,
> The Master's up and away,
> Hallo, hallo, we'll follow him through
> From Bratton to Porlock Bay.
>
> Knightacott, Narracott, Hurracott past,
> Straight for the north they race,
> He's leading them straight by Blackmoor Gate
> And he's setting a pounding pace.

They're running him now on a breast high scent,
But he leaves them standing still,
When they swing round by Westland Pound,
He's far on Challacombe Hill.

The pack's a string of struggling ants,
The quarry's a dancing midge,
They're plying the reins on the edge of the Chains
While he's on Cheriton Ridge.

He's gone by Kittuck and up (Lu)cott Moor,
He's gone by Woodcocks Ley
To the little white town he's turned them down
And he's soiling in the open sea.

So hurry along, we'll both be in,
And the crowd's a parish away,
We're a field or two and we followed him through
From Bratton to Porlock Bay.[15]

J. M. W. Turner RA (1775-1851) came of a North Devon family. His father was a barber in South Molton and his uncle was workhouse master in Barnstaple. There are still collateral descendants in the area.

Turner made a West Country sketching tour in the nineteenth century. He painted and drew some wonderfully striking maritime subjects. Amongst his Somerset and North Devon coastal scenes, Turner depicted Watchet Harbour, Minehead (with Dunster in the foreground), 'Comb' Martin, 'Ilfracomb' and Clovelly (from Bucks Mills), which is misnamed as being in Somersetshire in my print. It was a great pity he did not paint Lynmouth or Woody Bay.

In the Ilfracombe picture Turner displays a sublime treatment of the raging sea whirling and twisting with savage disregard for man, for, on close inspection, tiny figures are seen clinging to the mast of a near sunken boat. Lilliputian creatures climb up (or down to the rescue) the steep cliff face where more people are waiting on the top. The lowering skies, the barren rocks and the threatening waters set in diagonal lines converging on Ilfracombe all combine to make this portrayal a most awesome seascape.

Philip Gosse was a painstaking nineteenth century naturalist working at the time when Darwin's revolutionary theories, which he publicly challenged, were being explored. Gosse was a marine zoologist and writer of natural history of some distinction. He was an old-fashioned member of the Plymouth Brethren and a lay preacher. He lived in South Devon for some years and spent nine months exploring the coasts of North Devon while staying in Ilfracombe. He, together with his small son Edmund, combed the beaches for specimens — at Braunton, Mortehoe, Lee, Ilfracombe and Combe Martin. These incursions are described in *A Naturalist's Rambles on the Devonshire Coast*. Philip Gosse went Medusa fishing in the Ilfracombe caves and his treatment of the jellyfish shows his sensitivity and gentleness. In his preface Gosse exhorts his reader:

> 'I venture to ask your companionship, courteous Reader, in my Rambles over field and down in the fresh dewy morning; I ask you to listen with me to the carol of the lark, and the hum of the wild bee; I ask you to stand with me at the edge of the precipice and mark the glories of the setting sun; to watch with me the mantling tide as it rolls inward, and roars among the hollow caves; I ask you to share with me the delightful emotions which the contemplation of unbounded beauty and beneficence ever calls up in the cultivated mind.'

A Naturalist's Rambles has one very beautiful paragraph:

> 'Farther on Trentistowe [possibly Trentishoe, the neighbouring parish to Woody Bay] displayed a similar combination of smiling fields and dark woods. The blue blossoms of the sheep's bit studded the banks, and there was a wall covered with the Convolvulus arvensis, in which the white flowers were so thick, that it looked as if a pall of green velvet had been thrown over it, studded with silver stars.'[16]

Philip Gosse unfortunately antagonized his son by his literal biblical faith and in later life Edmund Gosse wrote an excellent but adversely critical biography of his father entitled *Father and Son*.[17]

The Orchard Theatre is North Devon's own professional company. It is now based in Barnstaple but takes its plays on tour to small theatres, halls and churches around the county and the whole of South-West England. The company mostly presents plays with a West Country flavour. Its actors change, but for four years until 1988 the artistic director was the imaginative and sensitive Nigel Bryant.

In 1970 the Orchard Theatre performed *Cruel Coppinger*, a play about the legendary pirate who roamed the border coasts of North Devon and North Cornwall. In 1974 the company staged *The Dicky Slader Show*, portraying anecdotes from the life of the North Devonshire pedlar-poet. 1975 saw the talented Kenneth McClellan as the eccentric *Hawker of Morewentstow*, who was also the curate of Welcombe. This presentation was acted at Parracombe church amongst other places. In 1980 Donald McBride, who acted his characters with rare relish, featured in the one-man show *Bold Squire Arscott*.

Recent productions have included *The Lie of the Land* by Jane Beeson, *The Death of Arthur* and an evocative production of Hardy's *Tess of the d'Urbervilles*.[18]

Theatre-goers who frequent the productions of the Orchard Theatre reckon that at their best they are as thought-provoking, as well acted and as polished as those of London theatre companies.

From time to time BBC television presents programmes about the North Devon coast and Exmoor being areas of outstanding natural beauty with acres of wild, unspoilt moorland. For example, John Noakes of 'Blue Peter' was filmed in the seventies walking the North Devon Coast Path. He stopped at Lynton and several notable locals were portrayed in this production. Recently, there have been programmes about the vexed question of hunting the deer.

In 1976 a BBC play *Where Adam Stood*, about Charles Kingsley and Darwin, was televised. Half of the seaside shots were taken at Woody Bay where locals were used for extras. The play was excellent and it is hoped that it might be rescreened in due course with appropriate publicity in the West Country.

In a rural area rather bereft of theatres and concert halls, productions tend to be made by talented amateurs and are often performed in churches or stately homes. Rachel, my elder daughter, and I attended a delightful concert one evening in 1978 in the tiny grey stone church of Trentishoe. The latter is a nearby hamlet adjacent to Woody Bay. Bishop James Hannington was once curate here as well as to Martinhoe. The concert included the organ, harpsichord, cello, recorders and violin. It was songs of praise and for all the world like an old service led by those in the musicians' gallery which Trentishoe still retains.

The organ at Trentishoe was once that of the SS *Mauretania*, presented to the church by the Cunard Steam Ship Company in January 1966 after the liner's last Atlantic voyage. Mr Dick Turpin, the organist, played it for the first time one evensong.

On another occasion I took Mark, my elder son, and Rachel to nearby Combe Martin church, whose Far Eastern vicar was most welcoming, to hear two young musicians singing and playing the recorder and harpsichord under the Yehudi Menuhin 'Live Music Now' scheme. In the programme were works by Telemann, Dowland and Purcell.

An exciting troupe of musicians is the Exmoor Chamber Orchestra which is made up of talented local amateurs and professionals. In January 1989 they played the music of Purcell, Delius and Haydn in St Mary's Church, Lynton to a full and enthusiastic house.

Ted Hughes, the present Poet Laureate, lives at North Tawton near Dartmoor and has enjoyed fishing Exmoor waters. He was married to the elusive and allusive poet Sylvia Plath. Hughes gives occasional lectures to local schoolchildren and other groups which are strikingly untraditional in their manner and content. He writes mostly in blank verse and has produced some stunning and shocking word pictures.

Here are the last nine lines of 'Birth of Rainbow' from a collection of West Country poems about farm life in Devon.

Blobbed antiseptic on to the sodden blood-dangle
Of his muddy birth-cord, and left her
Inspecting the new smell. The whole South West
Was black as nightfall.
Trailing squall-smokes hung over the moor leaning
And whitening towards us, then the world blurred
And disappeared in forty-five degree hail
And a gate-jerking blast. We got to cover.
Left to God the calf and his mother.[19]

Two novelists have written engagingly about Woody Bay this century. They are Malcolm Elwin and E. Phillips Oppenheim. The latter wrote *Nobody's Man*, set in Woody Bay and Woolhanger, which fabricates an intriguing love-story between the two manor owners.[20]

During the war, when his daughter remembers seeing U-boats go up the channel, Malcolm Elwin, the well-known biographer and literary critic, lived at Little Raveley for five years. While he was there he wrote his rollicking murder-romance *The Little Hangman*. He and his family were tenants of the Bostocks who had built the house on the site of the Woody Bay Hotel croquet lawn in 1927.

The heroine of *The Little Hangman* lived at a house modelled on the Red House and Mrs Joyner the owner, Mr Edwin Richards's mother-in-law, suggested some characteristics of Mrs Alabaster. Dr Quick was based on Stanley Holman and Butcher Parr was more or less Bill Allison.[21]

Elkie Brooks is the artiste of Woody Bay in 1990. She is a pertinent and determined dark-haired little figure who may be seen alongside her handsome, fair, tall husband or with her two attractive dark young children. She is usually seen darting about the local shops or dashing up and down the road to the sea in one of her Range Rovers number-plated 'ELK'. Otherwise she may be spotted jet-skiing round Lynmouth Bay with the family.

Elkie has a mane of chestnut and copper-coloured hair through which her velvet brown eyes peer with reserve and then with increasing warmth while she is conversing. As the eye is so is the person.

Ten years ago Elkie and Trevor Jordan moved to Woody Bay. Obviously, living on the coast of North Devon is very different from being in the hub of a city like Manchester or London where they lived previously.

Elkie has been in the music business for thirty years: she scarcely looks old enough and all her experiences, together with the risks involved, have not aged her at all. She started singing at sixteen and says it has taken her long and difficult years to reach success. In the early days Elkie was affected by singers such as Cliff Richard, Elvis, Ella Fitzgerald, Sarah Vaughan and Billie Holiday. Now she is open to all kinds of influences and likes the kind of music that her son Jay likes, such as that produced by Michael Jackson.

Elkie's family was and is a musical one. Her mother's mother was a concert pianist, violinist and singer. Her father's brother, Nat Bookbinder, and his boys were all musicians. So were Elkie's two brothers. Her parents are very supportive and great fans: they have a large collection of Elkie's albums and pictures.

Trevor and Elkie have had a musical and marital partnership since 1978. They met at a concert where Diana Ross sang and for whom Trevor engineered the sound. Now Trevor engineers and produces many tracks of Elkie's discs. Together they write some of their own songs such as 'Sail on'. Elkie has greater ambition than merely selling discs. She wants to be in the charts and so gain acclaim thereby.

Mrs Trevor Jordan is a family and private person first and foremost. She says maybe she will have more time for socializing when she is older and less involved with her music and running her household. Jet-skiing is her great love as an exhilarating recreation. She also likes to a lesser extent her garden and wildlife; Trevor is more actively involved in these. Elkie is fond of cooking and one day hopes to produce her own recipe book.

The family love the peace and quiet and trees of Woody Bay and the surrounds of North Devon. The locals are friendly and the Jordans have the facilities for their hobbies at their disposal.

Woody Bayites feel a pleasure and a kind of pride as they switch on the radio to hear Elkie belting out in her inimitable husky voice the lines of a song like 'Sail on' which was recorded in the Woody Bay Studios at her house. 'Sail on' has both Christian overtones and lines reminiscent of the all-embracing sea along the local coastline:

I went down to the harbour to see the
    boat from Galilee
there she stood afloat in the brilliance
    of the sea, sail on —
sail on the water, sail on the sea
    sail on the water, sail on the sea — sail on by —

the sunset in the distance as she anchors
    in the bay
we all rowed out to greet her to
    see just how she lay, sail on —

sail on the water, sail on the sea

sail on the water, sail on the sea

never seen so many people they all seem
    friends of mine
there's never any violence never any crime
    everyone's so busy having such a good time
sail on, sail on, sail on —[22]

Ian Hudson, painter and singer, is a breezy, genial fellow with an 'open face': he looks people straight in the eye which perhaps comes from his spell as a salesman.

Ian has had no formal art training. He began painting bird studies when bored with his job: he sold these to his colleagues. Later, he went on to general wildlife subjects and portraits of domesticated pets, landscapes and, latterly, seascapes. He likes to work, mostly in water-colours, on a variety of themes.

Ian left Huishes at Taunton at fifteen and joined the Police Force in London for a short time. Then he had two years 'bumming around', working as a barman before going into salesmanship for about fifteen years. Eventually, Ian settled in a bank in London but he disliked the work and loathed commuting. He took up painting as a hobby.

In 1978 Ian and his wife Christine had a holiday at Combepark. The friendliness of the hotel and the locals endeared Ian to Exmoor and convinced him that this was where he would like to live. He moved to Furzehill the following year. He built himself a studio and began to learn his trade with the Brendon Art Group as the main source of tuition.

Ian paints what he likes now except when he is undertaking commissions. Then he gives the patrons just what they want. Such is the reputation he has built up that he has an annual exhibition in Minehead, Barbrook and Instow. In the 1989 Brendon Exhibition Ian showed his most ambitious work so far — a very large sea painting with unusual tints in the water and a striking old lugger as the centre-piece.

Ian is a folk-singer and he has a pleasant, mellow voice and he accompanies himself nicely on the guitar. He sings at the Woody Bay Hotel regularly in the summer. Ian also sings with the shanty group 'Heats of Oak' for fun and for charity. Recently, the 'Hearts of Oak' were featured in Harry Secombe's microscopic but delightful portrait of Exmoor in 'Highway' on television. Woody Bay and Ian Hudson share several connections. Certainly the hamlet is glad to be associated with such a very competent and imaginative Exmoor artist.

Below is an evocative poem by my daughter Deborah. It is a simple, childish piece of writing by a sturdy ten-year-old containing hope and a dream.

My home

My bedroom is small,
I sleep on a bunk,
My furniture's all
just covered in junk.

The kitchen's below,
The drawing-room's near,
Dad's next door.
So there's someone who'll hear.

if the piano I play,
or I stamp on the floor,
When I'm making my way,
from my desk to the door.

it's quite nice to be,
in our Woolhampton flat,
yet I don't feel I'm free,
when I'm there for all that.

But there is somewhere else,
that I think of as heaven,
a little sea-cottage,
in Northernmost Devon.[23]

In May 1990 an ambitious Festival of the Arts and Countryside based on Lynton, Lynmouth and Exmoor was held.

There was theatre comprising three most interesting pieces. These were the much-acclaimed Braunton School version of 'The Ancient Mariner' directed by Janet Cotter; a more local and movingly understated look at *Thirty Seven Years Ago*, written mainly by Lyn Withers, which detailed the terrible flood disaster in 1952 in which folk who were there and witnessed the disaster took part, including the Pedder family who performed particularly well; and the Orchard Theatre's new play *It came from under the Earth* about the archaeology, history, myth, legend and art of Exmoor.

The Festival also included Exmoor or West Country music, poetry, talks, exhibitions, films, spirited Carnivals and a special Service in St Mary's, Lynton. Guided walks were undertaken such as Coleridge, Lorna Doone and Williamson trails, as well as historical, natural history, coastal and archaeological walks conducted by the Exmoor Natural History Society, the Exmoor National Park, the Devon County Council, the Henry

Williamson Society, the National Trust and the Exmoor Society.

A beautiful week's weather helped to attract visitors and locals to the Festival, but another year, earlier increased publicity might draw more folk to the spectacular Lyn Valley.

References to Chapter Six

1. *The Exmoor Handbook and Gazetteer* N. V. Allen (1972) Exmoor Press.
2. *Coleridge and Wordsworth in Somerset* Berta Lawrence (1970) David & Charles.
3. *West Country Poems by Wordsworth and Coleridge* Richard J. Hutchings (1979) Hunnyhill Publications.
4. *Coleridge at Nether Stowey* R.F. (1972) The National Trust.
5. *The Complete Poetical Works of Percy Bysshe Shelley* (1907) OUP.
6. *A Shadowed Man: Henry Williamson* Lois Lamplugh (1990) Wellspring.
7. *West Country Verses* Arthur L. Salmon (1908) William Blackwood & Sons.
8. *Poems of T. E. Brown* (1915) MacMillan & Co., Ltd.
9. *Jennifred And Other Verses* Septimus G. Green (1899) Elliot Stock.
10. *Westward Ho!* Charles Kingsley (1923) J. M. Dent & Sons Ltd.
11. *Charles Kingsley: His Letters and Memories of His Life* edited by His Wife (1888) Kegan Paul, Trench & Co.
12. *Prose Idylls* Charles Kingsley (1873) MacMillan & Co., Ltd.
13. *Henry Williamson — a Portrait* Daniel Farson (1982) Michael Joseph Ltd.
14. *On Foot in Devon* Henry Williamson (1933) Alexander Maclehose & Co.
15. *Exmoor Custom And Song* P. W. Patten (1974) Exmoor Press.
16. *A Naturalist's Rambles on the Devonshire Coast* P. H. Gosse (1853) John Van Vorst.
17. *Father and Son* Edmund Gosse (1907) William Heinemann Ltd.
18. Programmes of the Orchard Theatre (1975-88).
19. *Moortown* Ted Hughes (1979) Faber & Faber.
20. *Nobody's Man* E. Phillips Oppenheim (1921) Hodder and Stoughton Ltd.
21. *The Little Hangman* Malcolm Elwin (1953) MacDonald.
22. *bookbinder's kid* 'sail on' elkie brooks/trevor jordan (1988) legend music group ltd.
23. 'My home' Deborah McMullen (Autumn 1983).

General

The Romance of The Men of Devon Francis Gribble (1912) Mills & Boon Ltd.

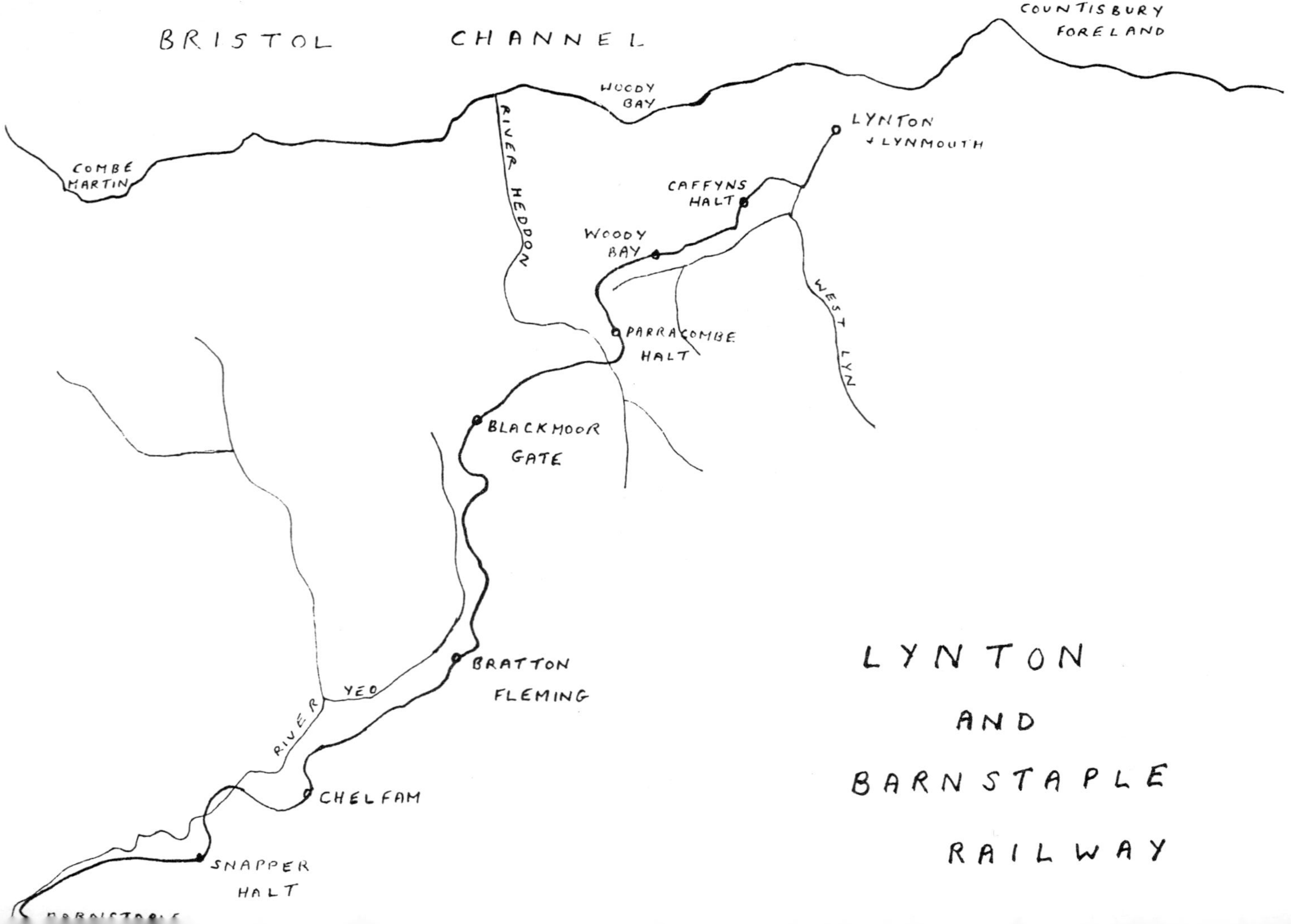
BRISTOL CHANNEL
COUNTISBURY FORELAND
WOODY BAY
COMBE MARTIN
RIVER HEDDON
LYNTON + LYNMOUTH
CAFFYNS HALT
WOODY BAY
WEST LYN
PARRACOMBE HALT
BLACKMOOR GATE
BRATTON FLEMING
RIVER YEO
CHELFAM
SNAPPER HALT
LYNTON AND BARNSTAPLE RAILWAY

CHAPTER SEVEN

THE LYNTON & BARNSTAPLE RAILWAY

In 1895 the Lynton and Barnstaple Railway Company, of which Sir George Newnes, the well-known Lynton benefactor, was Chairman, received the royal assent to construct a branch line from Lynton to Barnstaple. The gauge was to be 1 ft. 11½ in. Sir Thomas Hewitt, Colonel E. B. Jeune JP (whose wife was lady of the manor) and Mr W. H. Halliday were made directors. Sir James Szlumper was the consulting engineer. Mr Francis (Frank) William Chanter (brother of the Company's solicitor) was appointed engineer and he drew up the plans for the railway line. The line was to be used for goods as well as passengers. A tender of £42,100 by Mr James Nuttall of Manchester was accepted by the board. Mr R. Jones of Jones Bros., Lynton was given the contract to build the stations of which he actually built three — Lynton, Wooda Bay and Blackmoor Gate. Lady Newnes cut the first turf for Lynton station in 1895.

When it was finally complete there were six stations on the Lynton and Barnstaple railway line. These were Barnstaple, Chelfham, Bratton Fleming, Blackmoor Gate, Wooda Bay and Lynton. There were also three halts — at Snapper (opened in 1903), Parracombe, and Caffyns (1907). The line of 19½ miles ran through the most picturesque scenery of woodland, moorland, farmland, seascape and attractive North Devon towns and villages. The journey took at least 1½ hours. Wooda Bay was the summit of the railway at 1,000 ft. above sea-level. The line was opened by Sir George and Lady Newnes on 11 May 1898. Local dignitaries at the opening ceremony included historian Sydney Harper and Mayor C. E. R. Chanter of Barnstaple, who was also the Railway Company's solicitor. Lady Newnes cut the tape to allow the first train to enter Lynton and Lynmouth station. Appropriately, members of the lifeboat crew in uniform were standing aloft the signal-box to watch.

Brown, Prideaux and Radcliffe who wrote the standard *Lynton and Barnstaple Railway* in 1964 recorded that the company travelled along the line before the official opening. On the pre-opening run the overloaded locomotive, which was pulling four coaches, failed at Wooda Bay and the party had to finish their journey by horse-drawn coaches to the Valley of Rocks Hotel, Lynton, for a luncheon engagement.

There was a deep cutting beyond the Wooda Bay station and the main road crossed the line here. Some yards farther on the Woolhanger lane also bridged the cutting.

The Lynton and Barnstaple Railway was a grand feature for isolated Wooda Bay to have in its vicinity. Caffyns Halt, one of the stops just inland of Wooda Bay, boasted a golf-course. (There was also one in the field containing tumuli immediately to the west of the top Wooda Bay car-park.) It is now likely that the Caffyns Golf-Links will be restored.

The infamous Benjamin Greene Lake had wanted a branch line built from Wooda Bay station to the projected new spa resort of Wooda Bay three miles to the north-east. In 1895 Colonel Lake agreed to let the directors of the Lynton & Barnstaple Railway Company site the Wooda Bay station at Martinhoe Cross on his land free of cost. In exchange, Lake was allowed to make a junction there for his branch line to Wooda Bay and to use the Wooda Bay station, possibly rent free. But the plan never materialized along with other schemes of his due to his financial difficulties. Thus, although there was 'an omnibus to and from the Glen Hotel to meet the principal trains', the Wooda Bay station mainly catered not for the hamlet of the same name but for the adjacent Station Hotel. Around 1905 Princess Christian and Princess Victoria came to the station here.

There were winter auction sales of livestock at Wooda Bay for which special up trains were run, leaving at 3 p.m. twice monthly, usually on Mondays.

In 1900, during the worst storm in the lifetime of the railway, the line was closed for several days. There were deep snow-drifts at Wooda Bay. On one occasion passengers were ferried from Wooda Bay to Lynton by the Jones Brothers' four-horse coach.

Storms, animals on the track, steep gradients, little used stations and halts all helped to make the Lynton & Barnstaple railway uneconomical.

In 1901 the name of the Wooda Bay station was changed to Woody Bay station in line with the official renaming of the Bay. It is believed that Woody Bay station, which looks very similar in construction to Blackmoor Gate and Lynton stations, originally had the same internal plan as the latter two. The Woody Bay station is slightly smaller than that of Lynton and Blackmoor. Whereas Woody Bay station formerly had an open yard on the north end, the other two had a large refreshment room. Also the Woody Bay station divided its official functioning area differently from Blackmoor and Lynton. Woody Bay had a large booking hall backed by an equally large office. The other two stations had a big general waiting-room and a small ticket office, and large refreshment rooms instead of the scullery which replaced the open yard at Woody Bay. All three had a ladies' waiting-room.

The Lynton and Barnstaple Railway (1964) contains the following amusing anecdotes about the line. One of the station-masters at Woody Bay, who was very fond of 'his pint and his gardening', telephoned to Pilton to ask staff there whether 'mumble-mumble', the general manager was coming to his summer hut in the grounds of the Woody Bay Hotel before he (the station-master) would have a drink or 'slipped off to his garden on a Friday'. Another story relates how a Lynton man would walk to Woody Bay on a Sunday, collect an inspection trolley left there for him during the week, put it on the track and, together with his wife and young daughter, race back home on it with a piece of wood for a brake. (This shows the steep gradient downwards from Woody Bay to Lynton.)

A local builder, Frank Hobbs of Lynton, with a characteristic chuckle, told a story about travelling on the Lynton & Barnstaple railway as a boy. He had jumped out of the first carriage, quickly picked some wild flowers from the banks and then jumped into the rear carriage, all while the train was moving. Such was the speed of the railway! The trains usually travelled at 15 miles an hour and a good average on the straighter runs was 22-23 miles per hour. The Light Railways Act specified that trains were not allowed to go faster then 25 m.p.h.

In 1923 the London and South Western Railway Company (becoming part of the Southern Railway Company in 1924) purchased the LBR. In 1935, after suffering the heavy loss of £100,000, the SRC decided to close the line. The company disclosed that there had always been a loss of at least £5,000 a year since it had bought the railway. There was dismay amongst many locals and other travellers. There were at least two appeals to the original Act referring to the Company being bound to maintain the line and 'for ever efficiently maintain' Woody Bay station.

The Lynton delegation who tried to halt the final closure travelled to a meeting in Barnstaple with the railway's general manager and Sir Basil Peto, the local MP — by car! One member, Mr Tom Floyd, did travel by train. Postman Tom was a much respected and much loved member of the community and was a Lynton Urban District councillor. His daughter, Mrs Jenkins, now living in Garson House, Lynton, speaks warmly and poignantly of her 'dear old Dad'. Years later, in 1952, a terrible tragedy was to strike (but not lastingly blight) his life. For on that night of August 15th he was to lose six of his family. Mrs Jenkins recounts awesomely how, from the doorway of her nearby cottage, as her father was being swept away down the road along with others, she managed to grab him 'by his braces' and thereby save his life.

To return to the railway, it is clear that, at the opening and closure of the LBR, it was expedient for its backers to use methods of transport other than the train on the narrow gauge line to travel (for at least part of the journey) to and from Lynton to Barnstaple. With hindsight, it is a great pity that all efforts to keep the railway alive failed, for had the LBR continued, most likely it would have been a tremendous tourist attraction after the Second World War.

At the sad demise of the LBR, it was a Woody Bay resident who sent the wreath to the station-master at Barnstaple on the day the last train ran on 29 September 1935. On it was inscribed 'In loving memory'. On one side of the attached card was written 'To Barnstaple and Lynton Railway With regret & sorrow From a constant user and admirer'. On the other side were these words with their biblical and Shakespearian overtones, 'Perchance it is not dead but sleepeth.' This extravagant token of bronze chrysanthemums was made by Paymaster Captain T. A. Woolf OBE, RN, (Retd.) who lived at the White House at Woody Bay. At a short ceremony photographed by R. L. Knight the station-master, Mr H. C. Ford, poignantly placed it around the lamp on the stop-block at the end of the line.

The track and stock were sold on 13 November 1935 and the station buildings on 7 October 1938 at the closing auction sale of the Lynton & Barnstaple Railway. Woody Bay station fetched £425 and it became a private house which it remains, unspoilt, to this day. Mr James Broom bought Blackmoor Gate station for £700. He built the adjacent Blackmoor Gate Hotel which was burnt to the ground in 1970.[1-13]

Henry Williamson left at least two descriptions of the Lynton & Barnstaple Railway. The first occasion quoted here tells of a happy family outing:

> It was Margy's fifth birthday and for her treat we planned to go to Lynmouth for the day, where among other things a prominent notice-board said 'Shelley's Cottage Bed and Breakfast'.
>
> The miniature railway from Barum to Lynton would soon be closed, for few used it nowadays, it took twice as long as the omnibus, though it was four times as nice to travel in. The children had never travelled on the train, so it would be their first and last time.
>
> Margaret, John, Windles, his friend Sleeboy, A'Bess, and I stood on the platform at the beginning of our journey and inspected the miniature engine.
>
> "Cor, look at the high funnel," said John.
>
> "I say, look Sleeboy, it's got a cow-catcher, but I suppose it's for the red deer, and what a huge dome — I bet it takes the driver a long time to polish it every morning," said Windles, whose job it was every Saturday to shine the brass door handles at home.
>
> * * *
>
> The train followed the deep wooded valley of the River Yeo, on the up-grade all the way. Through hail and rain the valiant little engine hauled us, past fields, vague and grey and suddenly a brilliant green, everywhere streaming with water. Then an excitement: it stopped. The driver and fireman alighted and walked forward. Heads peered out of windows. The driver returned with a lamb under his arm. Margy purred with sympathy. The lamb was put over the wire fence, restored to its frantic ewe.
>
> "Why didn't we use the cow-catcher?" grumbled Windles. "Instead of stopping the train?"

"You croo' little boy, you!" cried Margaret, adding, with a quick glance at me: "It's my birthday party, not yours!"

Just before slowing up for Lynton the rain began to fall heavily and we were glad of our raincoats, brought reluctantly by the children and bundled on the wooden rack over our heads.

We walked down the steep stony track to Lynmouth and after some ginger beer at an inn at the foot of Sinai Hill, we ate our sandwiches in the shelter of a baker's porch, while the rain lashed down. After a three hours' exploration of the beach in the rain, we took the funicular carriage up the cliff to Lynton and climbed to the station again. The railway company had given me a free pass, and so on the return journey I got into the first-class coach, a luxurious pullman made almost entirely of glass. "A proper toff is our father," remarked Windles. From their carriage came shouts, hoots, whistles, and exhortations to the driver to "make her spark". For ninety minutes they kept up their racket. What vitality![14]

The second account is from *How dear is Life (A Chronicle of Ancient Sunlight)* in which Williamson details the LBR train ride in the life of a boy going on holiday to stay with his aunt in Lynmouth.

The river widened into sudden sullenness. It moved slowly, with scum on it, under oakwoods which came down to its steep sides, as muddy as the reaches of the Thames when the tide was out. Could they be near the sea? He leaned out of the window, and saw, faintly under the spiky western sun, a pale length of sand with heat-hazed hills beyond. This must be Barnstaple! He put bag and rod on the seat before him, alert with excitement.

Aunt Theodora had written that he must stay in the train until the second stop, at the town station; and then change to the small-gauge Lynton train he would see awaiting the London train on the opposite platform. It would take almost two hours to Lynton, but the country was very beautiful, she said. Sylvia would meet him at the Lynton station, if she was not able to come herself and bring him down to the cottage.

He got into the miniature Lynton train. The engine looked like a green oblong tank, with a red cow-catcher in front. It had a big polished brass dome like an immense fireman's helmet rising out of the middle of the tank. There were only three carriages, one of them almost all made of glass, the first-class one. He got into a third, and stared about him, at the swans in the river, wooden ships moored at the quay on one side, and the number of traps and carts drawn by horses on the road seen through the opposite window. There was only one other person in his carriage, an old farmer with mutton-chop whiskers and a square sort of bowler hat on his head.

At last the tiny engine gave a discordant shriek of its twin brass whistles, and with much chuffing, and rattling of the carriage, started off. By the rapid chuffing it seemed to be racing, until by comparison with the people and houses outside it was seen to be creeping. The longer it took the better. To ride in such a train was an adventure which he would like to go on for ever.

The engine puffed and huffed out of the town, and up a green valley with oakwoods on either side, and meadows thick with rushes, where sheep and red cattle grazed. It passed over very small bridges, and left whiffs of steam through cuttings like a story-book train. Once it stopped, for a bullock on the line. He saw large birds soaring in wide spirals far above a hill, and counted seven one above the other, sailing serenely in the blue.

* * *

... the train had climbed away from the deep valley. From now on it ran through rocky cuttings and high embankments on which yellow furze bloomed, filling the carriage with its sweet smell. Bees wandered through the open window, like the butterflies of hours ago; long ago in the morning of the day whose eternity was now ending.

It was a dream country, floating on sunshine, the world lying far below. Were some of the shaggy men with dogs, drovers of cattle, descendants of the Doones? The train stopped at Black Moor Gate; in a drowse of steam he listened to strange words and voices of rough shaggy men with sticks in hand shouting at bullocks among barking shaggy dogs. All seemed to share one language. At last the stamping was finished, and with the cattle truck coupled, the train went on, crawling to Parracombe Halt. Thereafter views of the moor, purple above the far smooth azure Severn Sea; then a louder chuffing of Yuffing Yeo, or whatever the old engine was called, echoed from the trees of Wooda Bay — another name mentioned by Father, Little Wood Bay. They were now surely at the highest part of the moor. It was shimmering, with a shimmer of a bee's wing! Leaning out of the window, he gazed upon the calm grey-blue sea stretching to a layer of white bubbled clouds above a far land. Good lord, it must be Wales!

He had travelled a great distance to be within sight of Wales! He waved his arms, and jigged upon the carriage floor.

The last orange was eaten, the last glaze of the sun upon the sea was glimpsed, and then Yuffing Yeo was running down above the oakwoods of the Lyn valley, to the terminus on the side of the hill above the town. Alas, the journey was over. He said goodbye to his carriage, and to the valiant little engine that had pulled him to his destination; and got out, to the melancholy belving of cattle behind — and saw he was the only passenger.[15]*

The Lynton & Barnstaple railway was one of the longest small gauge railways in England and one of the most picturesque and famous in the world: as such it well deserves to be reopened.

By 1979 the enthusiastic Bill Pryor had bought the Lynton Station House and a small diesel engine of the same gauge as the original LBR engines and laid track for it in his garden. In that year he and others formed the Lynton and Barnstaple Railway Association. This was a real excitement for local railway enthusiasts and other sympathetic supporters. There were the dual aims of restarting the 1 ft. 11½ in. gauge Lynton & Barnstaple railway line where possible and of opening a museum of railway items. 'Perchance it is not dead, but sleepeth', but many locals, though fond of the old line, wagged their heads; one said, "Gude Laur' bless 'e, they'l nivver git et gwain agean, no nivver — vor ther' be tu many varmers agaens 't whu owns the land roun' yer 'bouts, m'dear!"

The stations and the halts were still intact in 1979 and so were many of the bridges, but none of the original track remained in place. The line, along with other small ones (for example, the Barnstaple-Bideford and the Barnstaple-Ilfracombe lines), was considered for a working tourist line or a major footpath. A high flying businessman from Brittany was keen to transpose his own small railway to a local line over here. But the Devon parties would have none of this. Unfortunately, there were disagreements within the LBRA and partly because of divided forces, it seemed, as my son concluded at the end of his O level history project on the Lynton & Barnstaple Railway (awarded 100%), it would be unlikely that the railway would ever be reopened (at least in its entirety).

However, the committee of the LBRA did in the early years make strenuous efforts to acquire plots of land on offer between Woody Bay station and Parracombe Halt and around Blackmoor Gate. They purchased one-third of a mile of the Parracombe stretch and in 1981 they began to clear rubble, and wire the trackside towards its restoration. They acquired stock and even started laying some track at Parracombe. But, in spite of local and railway buff enthusiasm, the fire of the first Lynton-based committees in practical terms came to little that was tangible.

The Lynton committee had a disagreement with the London group and then an argument between themselves which led to the Association and its officers, together with its new museum, being Barnstaple-based. The latter is attractively situated next to the old Barnstaple railway station (now a

*Both these extracts are reproduced by kind permission of the estate of Henry Williamson.

restaurant) and inside is crammed all manner of interesting articles.

The Association has acquired some rolling stock, several miles of track and one of the original turntables of the LBR from the Romney, Hythe and Dymchurch Railway, and two narrow gauge engines. It is seeking to bring back the elusive engine *Lew* after its many years' service in Brazil.

In mid-February 1990 the exciting news came that the North Devon District Council had agreed, by 20-3 votes, to the outline planning application from the Lynton and Barnstaple Railway Association for two to three miles of track between Silver Leat, Barnstaple and Snapper Mead, near Goodleigh. The main stumbling block was the suspected noise and pollution disturbance which critics reckoned would emanate from the railway. Rosy-cheeked Clarence de la Cour, the Association's chairman, was highly delighted that planning permission had been given for part of the railway to run again. But he warned that there were many challenges ahead. The LBRA urgently needs financial and practical backing to realize the dream of partial revival by its centenary.

It is clear that the present day management committee members of the LBR, together with its Association, are imbued with something of the spirit that endowed Sir George Newnes and his fellow innovators of the early years. Good luck and all strength to your elbow, LBR![16-18]

References to Chapter Seven

1. *The Lynton & Barnstaple Railway* L. T. Catchpole (1972) The Oakwood Press.
2. *The Lynton and Barnstaple Railway* G. A. Brown, J. D. C. Prideaux, H. G. Radcliffe (1971) David & Charles Ltd.
3. *Lynton and Barnstaple Railway Album* J. D. C. A. Prideaux (1974) David & Charles Ltd.
4. *The Lynton & Barnstaple Railway* J. R. Yeomans (1979) D. Bradford Barton Ltd.
5. *Portrait of the Lynton & Barnstaple Railway* Chris Leigh (1983) Ian Allen.
6. 'Articles of Agreement' between the Provisional Directors of the Lynton and Barnstaple Railway Company, and Benjamin Greene Lake (12.2.1895).
7. 'Particulars, Plans and Conditions of Sale of the Valuable Freehold Properties forming Part of the Lynton and Barnstaple Railway' H. L. Smedley, Solicitor, Waterloo Station, London, SE1 (1938).
8. *Railways Round Exmoor* Robin Madge (1971) Exmoor Press.
9. *Back Along the Lines: North Devon's Railways* Victor Thompson (1983) Badger Books.
10. *North Devonshire Railway Delights* Colin Henry Bastin (1988) C. H. Bastin.
11. *The Book of Lynton & Lynmouth* Eric Delderfield (1981) E. R. D. Pubns.
12. *North Devon Story* Eric Delderfield (1962) Raleigh Press.
13. *Murray's Handbook for Devon* (1895).
14. *The Children of Shallowford* Henry Williamson (1939) Faber & Faber Ltd.
15. *A Chronicle of Ancient Sunlight: How dear is life* Henry Williamson (1984) Macdonald & Co.
16. 'The Lynton & Barnstaple Railway Association newsletter' — various numbers from 1-14 (1979-84).
17. *The Lynton & Barnstaple Railway Magazine* — various numbers from 15-32 (1984-90).
18. *The North Devon Journal-Herald.*

CHAPTER EIGHT

LOCAL PERSONALITIES, PAST, PRESENT AND FUTURE

Although less sharpened by the bustle and deprivation of urban life, country dwellers often have a native wit which most likely comes from close contact and confrontation with open spaces, the land with all its lush vegetation, bare earth and rocks, the sky and, for those fortunate enough to live by them, rivers and the sea. Certainly, there have been some remarkable and resilient characters living and working in the Lyn Valley area.

Ursula Kay, sensitive and unassuming, was one such person, working at Lee Abbey for over 25 years until her death in 1984. The daughter of missionary parents in India and gaining her B.Sc. in geography and geology at London University, Ursula was a winsome and endearing Christian. The light of her faith shone through her life. She was a farmer, naturalist, gardener, writer, and an artist, and also the producer of one of the best cream teas in North Devon. She lived in the cottage-cum-café by the Lee Abbey toll hut, south-east inland from Crock Point. (In the 1930s a Mrs Delbridge had a tea-shop here where 'tea was served with wasps in the garden'.) In Ursula's time up to 500 scones were made daily at the cottage in the season. Wasps occasionally made their appearance at Ursula's teas amidst her brilliant show of shrubs and flowers. But (as at Watersmeet), more commonly, attractive garden birds would alight unabashed on visitors' tables to demolish with greedy beaks any tempting scraps.

Interestingly, in 1984 Ursula, on a scramble down to Crock Pits Beach (Woody Bay), found that 'a recent rock fall had exposed (once more) some of the china clay which used to be mined here in the eighteenth century'. At Lee Bay Lee Abbey has made a small museum in memory of Ursula, housing a number of her finds and records of the area including natural history specimens, photographs, drawings, maps, writings and other data. It is a celebration of Ursula.

Another colourful character, well known to a number of folk at Woody Bay, was the arresting and genial (despite much pain at the end of his life) Frank Hobbs. Frank was a Lynton builder. He did a lot of reconstruction work after the Lynton and Lynmouth flood disaster in 1952, and undertook attractive and colourful stone work and necessary and welcome repairs, refurbishments and extensions to houses in Woody Bay. He was a ready friend to all and spontaneously sympathetic to those in trouble. Frank's genuine friendliness was renowned and he was chosen to portray a typical Devonian of the locality when John Noakes produced a film about coastal paths for BBC Television. Frank's warm Devonshire accent came over as

August 1983

Lynton builder dies at 67

LYNTON builder Frank Hobbs has died, aged 67. But his name will live on, carved secretly in scores of stone fireplaces and other work of which he was proud.

Mr. Hobbs's firm built stone walling across Barnstaple and Bideford bridges and he was responsible for much reconstruction work after the 1952 Lynmouth Flood Disaster.

He retired from running his own firm over ten years ago, but spent many hours working with his two sons, Bill and Brian, in their building businesses.

Won award

Extensions to Lee Abbey, which won a "Financial Times" award, were also his work.

Mr. Hobbs went into business after the war with his brother, Jack, who later started his own building firm in the town. For many years he played for Lynton soccer and cricket clubs, later serving as an official and still umpiring last summer. His sons and grandsons have now followed him into the clubs.

He was closely associated with Lynton Parish Church and had been a churchwarden.

Mr. Hobbs lived at 5, Belle Vue Avenue and died at Lynton Cottage Hospital after a short illness. He leaves a widow, Edith, their two sons and a daughter, Jean, who is married to Bideford soccer player and coach Peter Druce.

no one else's could. When he died in 1983 Frank left many friends the poorer. He was someone who was larger than life. Frank left a widow, Edith, two sons and a daughter who all worked with him in the building trade at some time. Now his son, Brian Hobbs, runs the family building business.

If Frank was of the earth and land Bob Jones, with his equally handsome weather-browned face, smacks of the sea and boats on which he has spent a good deal of his life. His grandfather, also Bob, designed and built the Cliff Railway for Sir George Newnes which opened in 1890. His father, later the railway's engineer, added the safety brakes. Bob, the younger, in his turn was the Cliff Railway engineer and is now the managing director. He redesigned the bearings in 1971 and installed a 'new' top wheel in 1982 which saved time and money on the maintenance of the railway. (In 1896, the Jones Bros. tendered for the construction of the Lynton & Barnstaple Railway but, at £48,000, it was considerably higher than that of £42,100 which James Nuttall of Manchester, who finally won the contract, had submitted. However, Mr R. Jones did gain the contract to build the stations for the railway.) Bob has rubbed shoulders with Woody Bay inhabitants when they have used the funicular railway and have gone mackerel fishing with him. His kindness, shyness and quick humour have made him a great favourite with, and much appreciated by, local residents and visitors alike.

Robin Richards, ex-resident of Woody Bay, joined the regular army in 1939 and served as a Major in the Western Desert and Italy and worked at the War Office. He was also a renowned racing driver, a broadcaster for thirty-three years and a writer. The Red House, Woody Bay, had once belonged to Mrs Joyner, Robin's grandmother. His father owned the house until 1960. Robin was born in 1920 and he lived in Woody Bay as a child and a youth until 1939. All the family had left belongings there, and when they were sorting out the residue Robin and Anne, his wife, found a 4 ft. lizard skeleton and a crocodile, relics from trips abroad. When the Richards family left the Red House it was sold for £2,500.

Robin's sister, Elizabeth, works for the South American Missionary Society in Paraguay. She was set on being a missionary from earliest years. Her father was dead against it and it was only at the age of 30 when he died that her vocation could be fulfilled. She is now very committed. She is ten years younger than Robin and returns home every four years. She might well retire in Paraguay.

The Richards had warm milk from not necessarily clean churns from Farmer Ridd delivered in a horse and trap. The postman, Antel, came from Parracombe on a donkey or pony with sacks either side. After his deliveries, he went to a little stable hut which was on the right of the last sharp bend on the beach road down to Woody Bay Cottage, where he ate sandwiches and gave his pony hay. Then he collected the outgoing mail.

'100 steps' directly below the Red House led through the trees to the postman's hut. I have since investigated this path (and others near by) myself. It was parallel with a stream running downwards to join the Hanging Water Fall. Then the path continued alongside the cascade over the headland to the shore. A right-hand fork in the tracks beneath the Red House led directly to the cliffs. These routes are mentioned by Malcolm Elwin in *The Little Hangman*. The shorter one, from which the heroine used to go bathing, leads straight to what is now a fallen away and crumbling cliff. Some of the steps, now mostly overgrown with vegetation, are still discernable. The Ordnance Survey map of 1903 shows these paths which were presumably cut by Colonel Lake (they are not given on the earlier OS map of 1888 before the Glen Hotel was built). The only uncovered stone steps to be found in the vicinity are a few cut up into the hillside off the path running over Inkerman Bridge from Trees to the Woody Bay Hotel, between the bridge and the hotel on the right-hand side. These were the start of a short path to the hotel. In this area at one time was a small café.

There was no mains electricity. Folk had paraffin stoves and Aladdin lamps. A few, like Stanley Holman, had generators. He made a reservoir upstream from Inkerman Bridge. The water was piped to the Woody Bay Cottage stone hut where the turbine was to make the hydro-electricity for the Manor House. Other houses in the Bay had different types of generators.

Stanley Holman, who had been at the Woody Bay Hotel since 1926 and owned both the hotel and the Manor from 1930 onwards, was a difficult character. Arthur Morgan Edwards was the proprietor of the Woody Bay Hotel from 1935-9 and had commissioned E. P. Leigh-Bennett's hotel brochure. Captain Tommy Broome RAF (Retd.) took over the Woody Bay Hotel (once the Glen Hotel) by 1945 and wanted to make it into something like a gambling den. His son painted attractive murals at the hotel. Putley, following Broome in 1950, wanted to attract Liverpool workers to a locality rather too quiet for them. Jurgen and Elisabeth Kempf made a success of the hotel in the early seventies before moving off elsewhere. Now, in 1990, they are running the popular quartet of inns, the Black Venus at Challacombe, Pyne Arms, East Down, Old Station House, Blackmoor Gate and the White Hart at Bratton Fleming.

Hawks Hill Cottage was once an outpost of the manor house, and the Coach House was stables, garages and staff accommodation for Glen Hotel. The main servants for the Manor were once Louie and Bill Marlow, who were the owners of Myrtle Cottage after Mrs Moysey living there from the twenties until the late sixties. Their son John was involved in a nasty accident while climbing up the cliff from the bottom of the slipway. His friend was killed and John sustained a severe hand injury. The crumbling cliffs in the area were to be respected and Robin termed Wringapeak a dangerous promontory with a knife edge.

At Slattenslade lived the only real Devonian, Horace Crang. At Martinhoe there were Ridds and Crocombes, Blackmores and Harrises. Margery Huxtable of Stock Farm, Furzehill, Barbrook, who worked manfully at Myrtle Cottage for a short time, was a Crocombe.

Mr Horace Crang, the one local Devonian (apart from the Mays) in Woody Bay, was born at Slattenslade Farm. He farmed there until he retired. His father, Charles William, and grandfather, Richard, owned Slattenslade before him. His great grandfather lived at Martinhoe. Percy B. May bought the farm from Horace's father in 1943. Horace is 78 and a cheery, contented character without outward regrets that the farm is no longer in the family.

Before the Smiths were 'lords' of the Manor Mr Crang knew Squires Bailey and Holman. Mr Holman, who he thought had owned the manor from 1925-39, was jealous of his privacy. He had put an iron bar on the road by Trees and one by the entrance to the old coast path in order to deny people their rights of way.

Horace told me he liked the Smith daughters ('all three good-looking girls'). Crang, a twinkle in his eye, likes to claim kinship with a one-time 'Lord of the Manor'. Years ago his relations, his grandfather, Richard Chaldon, and his uncle, Herbert John, worked Martinhoe Manor as a farm. They also had visitors and a public bar.

John Peak Crang lived at Wringapeak (once Seaview) before the Malets owned it. The Bostocks built Little Raveley in 1927 and holidayed there regularly until about 1939. (Mr Francis Charles Bostock was a bank manager in Taunton where his house was called 'Raveley'. His wife was Adelaide Bostock.)

Mr Crang said that the limekilns had not been worked since the turn of the century. He did not regret his lack of a sea view: he could see all the sea he wanted to from the brow of Woody Bay at Slattenslade.

At first the postie walked from Parracombe, then he came in a pony and trap. Thirty years ago there were two or three local traders delivering each day.

Crang recalled his 'Dad could mind the old coaches and horses.' Horace's abiding memory of the railway was that it was slow. Like most local Devonians, he is sceptical about it being reinstated because of the new landowners.

Horace touched on local wildlife. An interesting sight he had seen behind his home was a deer with three legs. Horace was *pro* hunting; he had found antlers at Woody Bay. Black grouse had been seen at Woolhanger.

Mr Crang said he thought Devon 'the best county', adding honestly that he had not travelled far to compare it to others much. Slattenslade comprised about 250 acres when he farmed it. He had mostly cows and sheep and less and less crops were produced. Subsidies were now good for farmers. The labourers were poorly off yet their lives were better than those of factory workers.

Robin and Valerie May gave me the following information about what is now their farm. After the war in 1945 Martinhoe Common, belonging to Slattenslade, was ploughed in response to the government's call for increased home food production and the heather converted to grass. It has been maintained as grass ever since. Corn, cabbages, swedes and turnips have all been grown on the in-bye ground of Slattenslade but now there are only swedes which are used as a winter feed for the ewe flock.

Martinhoe Common constitutes about half the 275 acres which make up the farm and is used mainly for summering the stock, whereas the in-bye ground, which is more fertile, is used for conserving hay and silage and for growing the crops.

Slattenslade Farm has been owned and run by a family company, set up in 1958, called the May Brothers, whose directors are the sons of Mr Percy May. A. Robin May, grandson of Percy May, took over Slattenslade in 1988.

Before Horace and his wife moved to Slattenslade Bungalow a casual labourer called Smyth had lived there. Slattenslade outbuildings were to become holiday homes, Crang thought.

There were once two farms at Slattenslade and a cottage or two. One was now ruined and one a stone shelter for animals — it had genuine domestic windows. Originally the cow barns were thatched.

On 21 October 1988 the Slattenslade animal houses were auctioned. It will be interesting to see to what use the new owner will convert them. If one of the cluster reverts to being a dwelling-house it has an original precedent, and should be pleasing to other Woody Bay residents who are keen to see the unchanging nature of Woody Bay retained.

John Oldham is a kindly retired flight lieutenant in the Royal Air Force. He lived at Martinhoe Rectory, the home of his grandfather the Revd Reginald Walter Oldham, with his father (who was in the Merchant Navy and away most of the time), his mother and his unmarried uncle and aunt during his most impressionable years. John was baptized at Martinhoe church (and also in Ireland where his mother's family lived). He attended the village school for several months. Lizzie and Tom Ridd lived in a white cottage near by. Lizzie was his father's nurse and Tom was their gardener. Lizzie Ridd moved to Beacon View on the Highveer road out of Martinhoe when she became a widow. The chief yeoman farmer in Martinhoe was John Ridd.

The three children of the Reverend Reginald Oldham were great tomboys and always scrambling over the cliffs. John's aunt, Marjorie, used to ride to dances in Lynton across the moors with her ball gown over her riding breeches. Later in her life she was a friend of Dora (Jill) Cartwright-Williams who was the owner-occupier of Little Raveley after the Bostocks sold the house; Jill moved to Little Raveley after the Lynton and Lynmouth flood in 1952 and lived there until 1979. (It was Jill who first instilled in me a deep interest in and a love for the written history of Woody Bay and its surrounding area.) Marjorie Oldham wrote four articles for the *Exmoor Review* in early editions.

John confirmed that the Holmans of the Manor and the Smiths after them both put up the Woody Bay gates to stop folk using the coast roads. The Woody Bay bathing pool was in a much better state earlier in the century. At Heddons Mouth, the next bay westwards approachable by road, Hunter's Inn (now re-built) — a lovely old thatched house — was burnt down, alas, in 1895.

John Oldham remembers visiting Mrs Moysey, a somewhat mazed, or touched, lonely widow at Myrtle Cottage. She would go off into peals of laughter for no apparent reason and John admitted ruefully that they could not but join in. But they laughed at her rather than with her because they did not know what she was laughing about.

Mrs Marlow, her housekeeper who inherited her property, was a wonderful cook (on old paraffin stoves) and later housekeeper to most of the Bay.

John reminded me that Mr Holmes, a London lawyer who delved in the occult, lived at Cherryford. His son, James Suttor Holmes, married Joan Harper of Robert Harper & Daughter, the excellent second-hand booksellers at Westward Ho! (now no longer there, unfortunately). Robert Harper was the son of Sidney Harper, the historian and printer, who wrote a children's *History of Barnstaple*. Joan Holmes first supplied me with second-hand books on this area and allowed me to photocopy numerous newspaper cuttings about the 'Woody Bay wars' and other local matters. She also let me borrow the catalogue of the Wooda Bay Building Estate Sale in 1900 and the 1930s brochure of the Woody Bay Hotel. Joan has since died but her brother, Robert, who was in the laundry business, lives in Appledore.

John Oldham, his spry and attractive wife Janet, and I discussed the pros and cons of the reopening of the Lynton & Barnstaple railway: John thought it impossible. The service had been slow and infrequent, for one thing, which deterred people from using it as a serious method of transport. John travelled on the railway and once, after travelling from Woody Bay to Blackmoor Gate, had a four-hour wait before there was a return train. Such was the infrequent train service (to what is, after all, a remote area).

The trains had pulled mixed carriages of people and goods. Once a coach full of passengers was left behind at Bratton Fleming by mistake while the engine and the rest of the train travelled on to Barnstaple. Workmen's trolleys, given a shove, ran down the track from Woody Bay station to Lynton by themselves.

John and Janet Oldham spent their honeymoon at the Station Hotel (now Moorlands) and contracted food poisoning for their pains.

Benjamin Greene Lake was John's father's godfather. He angled for an abortive branch line, two or three miles out to Wooda Bay proper, in the event of which the Wooda Bay station would become Martinhoe Cross. The Wooda Bay station-master was Mr Mills. The train ran under a bridge at Caffyns Halt where there was a road running down the valley to Outovercott (now a riding stables) which was owned by Malet, a Bath solicitor.

From life in the rectory we move on to a life spent working in a surgery. A local doctor, E. H. Mold, has made a special study of the Lynton area about which he has written a very interesting history called *Lynton and its Coast*. As yet it is unpublished.

Dr Mold has a lovely story about a visit of the Bishop of Exeter to Martinhoe Rectory which reminded me of tales of a bishop visiting Parson Froude at Knowstone. But this tale does not have a malicious core, merely a pragmatic thrust. The rector, Bertram E. Venton, lived in a rectory which was full of dry rot. Before being invited to tea the bishop was informed that the floor boards were liable to collapse. Everything was ready, but the path to the repast did not run in a straight line and of course, as was planned, he fell through the floor and Venton's point was brought home.

The Glen Hotel, later becoming the Woody Bay Hotel, was opened, Dr Mold thought, in 1893. It did well though the refreshment rooms on Inkerman Way have vanished. Passengers disembarking from steamers at the Woody Bay pier were taken up the hill by suitable vehicles.

Dr Mold believed that Squire Bailey, who bought the Wooda Bay Estate in 1900, had built Duty Point Tower in the nineteenth century to see what was passing in the Channel. He kept a good store of whisky there.

When some owners of the Manor put up a gate across the coast road to deter the use of it, they eventually offered keys to Dr Mold and his partner Dr Nightingale, the local doctors at the time. These they indignantly refused!

In the old days a surgery was held in the rectory at Parracombe when Kell was rector. Dr Mold has served Lynton and Lynmouth and the surrounding villages for nearly 30 years — from 1953-82.

Ernest Mold owns copies of C. H. Archer's 'Coastal Climbs in North Devon' of 1959, 1962 and 1963/1965 which are for private circulation only. With these is an interesting map drawn by the author, based on an Ordnance Survey map. It shows two of Hannington's paths both going down to Bloody Beach east of Highveer, the eastern one ending at Clinnock Hole near Hubert's Grotto (Archer's 'Big Cave'). It is proving more difficult to locate Cave Scriven. Archer tells of various exciting climbs between Woody Bay and Heddon's Mouth.

Dr Mold is renowned for his dinghy sailing and has probably hugged more of the local coastline than anyone else, except the Lynmouth fishermen and professional boatmen. Ernest Mold is an elder statesman in Lynton. He has done the town and her sister, Lynmouth, a great service by initiating their twinning with the French town of Benouville.

Dr Sydney Woodhouse, one-time owner of Woody Bay Cottage, is a splendidly white-haired stalwart 96-year-old who still enjoys walking, cooking and travelling around the world. After leaving the Royal Navy he worked at St Thomas's Hospital from 1920-60, for the last twelve years of which he was visiting consultant to Wandsworth and Brixton Prisons. Dr Woodhouse worked in Harley Street for twenty years. He retired at seventy and has continued to live a full life ever since.

Dr Woodhouse has his own views on the ill-fated Colonel Lake who was a solicitor with a Territorial decoration and owner of the manor. In the 1890s Lake built a pier. He hoped paddle-steamers would call plying between towns in South Wales and Ilfracombe and Barnstaple. (He wanted to make Woody Bay into a second Ilfracombe and, hoping for a fortune, he used other people's money to this end.) He cut a road down to the pier, pushed out the land on to the rocks for the approach to the landing-stage and established a bridge at the bottom of the road to the beach.

After three years there was a south-westerly gale. The planks in the pier probably had not been bored with holes as they should have been to allow uprising water to seep through. The gale of 1900 lifted the top of the pier off into the sea and that was the end of it. It was not, however, the end for Lake who was prosecuted and imprisoned. Dr Woodhouse agreed with most other past and present residents in Woody Bay that it was a good thing that Lake's schemes failed and that the Bay did not become another North Devon seaside town.

The oldest building in the Bay (excluding Slattenslade) is Woody Bay Cottage. It used to comprise two semi-detached cottages and they were 'pretty derelict' in the thirties, with a leaking roof. Dr Woodhouse and his brother, who was a South Molton solicitor, rented the cottage in the summers of 1933 and 1934. Dr Woodhouse bought the cottage in 1935.

Mr Holman was the owner of Martinhoe Manor and Woody Bay Cottage, and when the Woodhouses were first staying at the cottage he was engaged in a lawsuit: he had erected an iron gate by Woody Bay Cottage. A young woman came to collect sixpences there for access to the beach. The local council and residents rebelled. The case went to the Winchester High Court. Holman lost and it cost him £500.

Dr Woodhouse made an offer of £500 for Woody Bay Cottage and this was accepted. As well as making other improvements the doctor had the dry rot taken out. (It is a wet fungus which grows in sheets in the woods and he believed that workmen could carry the infection from one house to another by carrying the spores on their tools.)

The Woodhouse family had some very good holidays at Woody Bay Cottage where they rejoiced in their outstanding view. They used to take the train from London to Barnstaple in the war. From Barum they caught a bus to the top and walked the two or so miles over the moorland with their baggage to Woody Bay. The doctor also had friends and relations who had spent their honeymoon at the cottage.

During World War II there was no restriction on Woody Bay: there was no barbed wire to negotiate, although there was tar washed up on the beaches from sunken ships. After the fall of France planes came over the Woody Bay cliffs to bomb Swansea and Cardiff. It was thought that there were local spies giving them night directions.

After the war the roads in Woody Bay deteriorated. The path to the beach was badly broken up and it was easy to have an accident there and fall down to the beach.

The Woodhouses fished with lobster-pots which they sometimes pulled up at midnight. They put pots round the base of the pier. Dr Woodhouse averaged a lobster a day. One doctor friend went fishing inland at Woolhanger.

The bathing was good if care was taken with the currents. The spring tides whisked out very fast. The bathing pool had suited the children very well.

Woody Bay was wet — which made it so beautiful. Exmoor compares with the Lake District for rainfall: both places receive up to 80 in. a year.

Between the wars there was only a handful of residences at Woody Bay. The farm or piggery, now Hawks Hill Cottage, was uninhabited. Miss Abrahams lived at Wringapeak and in the summer she brought down youngsters from Children's Homes to stay there. The Richards, a well-known family locally, lived at the Red House. Robin Richards now lives at Furzehill. At the White House there lived a man named Grey who brought a young wife down with him, his first wife having died.

Dr Woodhouse told me several funny stories about poor Mrs Moysey of Myrtle Cottage. She was a whimsical creature. One evening she had been invited to dinner by the Richards for 7.30 p.m. and she arrived at 9 p.m. The meal was spoilt, but she gave a charming explanation. On her way up the path through the trees she had spotted glow-worms in the hedge and had been so taken with them that she had been unable to tear herself away.

On another occasion Mrs Moysey had invited the Holmans to a meal. This had been poor and, half-way through dinner, Mrs Moysey disappeared. After a while Mrs Holman went into the kitchen to see if she needed any help. There she found Mrs Moysey eating her sweet course all by herself quite oblivious of her guests in the next room.

Mr Holman called his wife 'Monkey' — she wore a little brooch depicting one. Mrs Moysey asked them for a meal and said, "I've got a special treat for you — champagne!" But it turned out to be only champagne cider after all, much to the disappointment of Stanley Holman who appreciated vintage wine.

Trees had an interesting history. It used to be Berry's post office and was called Woodcot at one time. At the start of the war it was sold for

£1,100, lock, stock and barrel. The owner was a retired sea captain who much improved it. A local builder brought up sand from the beach for repairs. Captain Temple-Grey collected pot lids which he had all over the house. When his wife died of cancer Temple-Grey decided to move to Berrynarbor. He advertised for another sea captain to share the house with him. It was on a hill with an outlook like one from a ship's bridge. Captain Temple-Grey was 'a bit neurotic' and kept a log (as he had a ship's) of his own health every day. The two captains took it in turns to pay the monthly bills. Temple-Grey was a very practical man and whatever he laid his hand to he improved. He sold Trees for a good price. Two sisters bought it and ran the house as a private hotel. Later they moved to Barnstaple.

Temple-Grey and others were in love with Woody Bay, but often found at last that the hard work involved in living there, the winters and the rain, caused them to move.

"Stanley Holman was a character," Dr Woodhouse said with a twinkle in his eye. He was 'pernickety' and insisted on his rights. When the owners of Trees wanted some timber felling in front of their house but on his property, to enlarge their view, Holman refused. (Such an undertaking was not carried out until the Jordans owned both residences.) Mr Holman died at Kentisbury Ford about 1946.

When Tommy Broome owned Woody Bay Hotel as well as Martinhoe Manor he only had a drinks licence for the hotel. He used to drive his guests from the Manor up Inkerman Way to the Woody Bay Hotel for a drink of an evening.

Mr Thornton who was one of the parsons of Martinhoe before the Second World War left a widow, with two sons, who later married a Canadian soldier. Mr Thornton's body lies under a grass mound, reputedly at his own wish, without a gravestone.

When he was at Woody Bay Dr Woodhouse and his eldest son found copper nooses in the woods set for deer and they would destroy these cruel traps. The land above the Bay had been heather and broom and there were curlew and red grouse up there which, sadly, have disappeared since the farmers were paid to grass the moorland. There was a Golf Club hut there which became derelict in World War II. Dr Woodhouse used to visit a Martinhoe farm for the odd fowl and dairy products during the war, and buy vegetables from a house near by. The doctor used to go out mushrooming on the hills around the Bay.

Newcomers to Woody Bay find the roads narrow and difficult especially in the season. By the White House there is a drop of 500 ft. Once Dr Woodhouse was forced off the road there with his wheels over the edge. His car had to be hauled back. But a car was a necessity in Woody Bay to prevent too much isolation.

The roads were somewhat better under National Trust ownership. The doctor said it was important that the gulleys should be kept clear as the surfaces of the roads were easily swept away. Although he was born in 1894 he had managed to walk to Lynton and back in 1985.

The Woodhouse family just missed the Lynton & Barnstaple railway operating. Dr Woodhouse said he thought the trouble with the economy of the line was that, in order to take the level route, it did not go through the villages. When the buses came they dropped people where they lived. He thought it would not pay to resurrect the railway.

In 1952 there were terrible floods in the area. Rain-water rose on the Chains and the moorland, unable to absorb any more, erupted in a vast spillage, swelling the rivers and causing a mighty deluge in Lynton and Lynmouth. 10 in. of rain fell in one day. Dr Woodhouse said that the burst dam at Woolhanger had contributed to the flooding. The bridge at the bottom of Woody Bay was blocked for weeks.

(In my cottage I have a much treasured fire-screen. It was given to my first husband, Terrence, and me by Jill Cartwright-Williams in memory of our son, Jonathan, whose rascally ways Jill loved. The wooden screen is the more precious because, set into its frame, are sixteen cracked English hand-painted Delft tiles. Jill's first husband, Francis, knew these intimately as he had been brought up with the screen. Ten of the tiles are of biblical scenes. There is Moses on Mount Sinai; one, I think, of Ruth harvesting; one of an angel appearing to two dismayed men; and one of Christ by the Sea of Galilee with his disciples casting their nets in its waters. The reason the screen is imperfect is because it was caught up in the Lynton and Lynmouth flood. While Jill and Frank sheltered, shivering in their bedroom, the waters swirled through their downstairs quarters, uplifting their furniture in the cottage where they lived at the time at Lyncombe.)

In 1958 the Woodhouses sold their cottage to Dr and Mrs Roger West of Bristol who modernized it a lot. Dr Woodhouse thought the Bay looked exactly the same as it had done when his family first came here, despite considerable improvements to a number of houses, and the views were just as they had been.

* * *

Now, in 1990, it is a good time to look back over a hundred years or more to the situation of Woody Bay before the Lake expansion, to consider the changes, to ponder what might have been, to review the present and look to the future.

During the first half of the nineteenth century there were only two dwelling-houses in Woody Bay proper, the old farmhouse which became Wooda Bay house, and Woody Bay Cottage. There were four residences in Slattenslade. Only a few families were recorded living in Woody Bay throughout the nineteenth century censuses. The families were mainly working on the land including lime-burning at the kiln, or were in service (the occupation 'servant' apropos of the Woody Bay area appears for the first time in the 1861 census).

The manor house stabling (now Hawks Hill Cottage) was probably built in the mid-nineteenth century, judging by the G. Rowe print of *c.* 1840 and the 1859 lease map on which it is not shown. During the time that Colonel Lake owned the Wooda Bay estate from 1885-1900, there were a further eight houses built (and also the pier and access roads). Little Raveley is the only twentieth century house.

The present occupants of the five houses open to visitors are in the service industry, and the residents of the remainder of the other twelve or fifteen have differing employment, with two out of three Slattenslade families still farming. There are no longer any Devonians in Woody Bay proper (excluding Slattenslade) and there has been a frequent change of residents during the twentieth century.

Colonel Lake essayed a burst of expansion in the 1880s and 1890s. But, because of his ineptitude with figures and heavy borrowing, not to mention embezzling, Lake's dreams of another Lynton and Lynmouth, or Ilfracombe at Woody Bay came to nothing.

Presumably, with more money of his own or with funds legally borrowed, Colonel Lake might have made Woody Bay into another flourishing little North Devon seaside town. But it is rather close to Lynton and Lynmouth. Also, 'instant' or 'purpose-built' resorts tend to lack charm and character compared with older places which have developed gradually. It is doubtful whether the steep sea cliffs at Woody Bay could be spoiled or less than spectacular, but the land above them could be desecrated.

Those of us who value Woody Bay today can be grateful to Benjamin Greene Lake, that he came, and went, leaving eight attractive Victorian houses and the remains of his Victorian dream.

We owe the arresting of Colonel Lake's expansion to Major Charles Frederick Bailey, who apparently was keen to conserve the beauty and unspoilt grandeur of Woody Bay. Had Lake been able to continue with his expansionist plans, he could have developed the whole of Woody Bay proper from Wringapeak Point on the west to Pines on the east and from the cliffs on the north, backed by the top road on the south as far as Slattenslade on the south-east. The area might have been covered with all manner of buildings which would have completely wrecked the lovely loneliness of the locality. Instead of a scattering of picturesque houses, there would be a purpose-built new town.

We may even be thankful that two World Wars restricted the extent and use of the money of entrepreneurs. After those momentous times the Exmoor National Park (which included Woody Bay) came into being in 1954. The Exmoor National Park Authority restrained unsuitable expansion within Exmoor. Finally came the National Trust to administer the Bay.

Happily, the National Trust, which is the custodian of much of Woody

Bay (as Lee Abbey has been entrusted with Lee Bay) and which bought it in 1965, should secure the Bay in its present state for the nation for centuries to come. As is the present trend, it would seem that the future lies in a reversion to something like the peace and quiet of the pre-Lake era.

As such, unspoilt (apart from some worrying pollution of the sea) Woody Bay is likely to hold its grand aspect, its sense of mystery and its changing colours for all lovers of nature, beauty and peace. Those who seek ephemeral sweetmeats and souvenirs, loud stereos and shops should look elsewhere! North Devon has some other marvellous seaside places along the coast, but Woody Bay is a strong contender for the crown, being still so natural and so little developed.

All of us who have come willingly to the Bay for greater or lesser periods of time have happily eschewed many city amenities and delights for that which far outweighs man-made joys — the spring and the summer, the soft sounds and the secrets of Woody Bay wildwood.

General Reference

A History of the Parishes of Lynton and Countisbury John Frederick Chanter (1907) James G. Commin.

Yesterday's Exmoor Hazel Eardley-Wilmot (1990) Exmoor Books.